the Ties that Bind

networking with style

the
Ties
that
Bind

networking with style

Danny Beyer

BookPress®
www.BookpressPublishing.com

Published in Des Moines, Iowa, by:
Bookpress Publishing
P.O. Box 71532, Des Moines, IA 50325
www.BookpressPublishing.com

Publisher's Cataloging-in-Publication Data

Names: Beyer, Danny Lee, author.
Title: The Ties That Bind : Networking with Style , second edition / Danny Beyer.
Description: Includes bibliographical references. | Des Moines, Iowa:
Bookpress Publishing, 2023.
Identifiers: LCCN: 2022945991 | ISBN: 978-1-947305-57-1
Subjects: LCSH Social networks. | Online social networks. | Success. | Leadership. | BISAC COMPUTERS / Internet / Social Media | BUSINESS & ECONOMICS / Business Communication / General | PSYCHOLOGY / Interpersonal Relations
Classification: LCC HM131 .B474 2023 | DDC307--dc23

First Edition
Printed in the United States of America
10 9 8 7 6 5 4 3 2 1

This book is dedicated to my incredible family.

Kacey, Isabella, and Tabitha -

none of this is possible without the love and

support of "my three ladies."

I love you to Betelgeuse and back!

CONTENTS

ACKNOWLEDGMENTS

Thank you to Susan Holden Martin for her time and commitment to this book. The professionalism and energy dedicated to this project made this edition better than I could have hoped for!

Thank you to Dr. Anthony Paustian for his friendship, guidance, and willingness to continue pushing me forward toward dreams I didn't realize I had.

Thank you to my parents, Dave and Linda Beyer, for continuing to show me how important relationships are to everything we do and who we become.

Thank you to the late Dale Groh. Without his willingness to give me an opportunity to shine and do things my way, none of this would have happened. I miss you, buddy.

And thank you to the countless others who have supported me in this process, allowed me to use their names and stories in this book, and provided counsel when I needed it the most, including:

Paul and Lynn Hays, JoAnn Morlan, Mitch Matthews, Adam Carroll, Zac Bale-Henry, Steve Chapman, Suku Radia, Mike Banasiak, Karla Walsh, Kate Banasiak, Kristin Runyan, Jann Freed, Jessica Susie, Gina David, Jay Byers, Raylee Melton, Justin Bogers, Dennis Markway, Greg Hayes, Kim Gratny, Daniel Willrich, Cindy Riesselman, Dr. Brett Vowles, Kyle Guldenpfennig, Erin Summers, Jim Summers, and Christopher Maharry.

CHAPTER 1

Using this Book

We need people. More specifically, we need relationships.

I originally wrote those words back in 2014 to open the first edition of *The Ties that Bind*. I knew in my soul that those words were true and provided facts and data to back them up throughout the remainder of the book. It turns out those words were even more true than I realized back then. Throughout the remainder of the 2010s and into early 2020, people and relationships pushed me forward both professionally and personally. The pandemic happened, and it seemed as if the entire world realized the power of connections and relationships overnight. We celebrated healthcare workers and sang across balconies. We figured out how to date with social distancing and held meetings online to keep things moving forward. As the world began to reopen, we started to reconnect. We watched videos of friends and families hugging after months, if not years, apart. There were tears and screams and dancing, and through it all, there were relationships.

I've debated updating this book for a long time, but there has always been an excuse to put it on the backburner. There are no more excuses, and now is the time. If the pandemic taught us anything, it is that time is precious and to take advantage of it.

One of the most significant changes in the second edition is that the companion workbook that was previously available by download through my website[1] is now included in the book. At the end of each appropriate section, you will find activities and exercises to get you working immediately on your networking. Feel free to use these workbook pages as you go through your first read or come back to them after you've completed the book. I believe they provide an additional resource that will serve you well for years to come.

We've changed as a society as technology has jumped forward ten-plus years to keep up with the new demands of digital conversations and meetings. I've been called multiple times in the last year to help colleges, businesses, and individuals re-enter the world and network in an even more connected world. Many of the messages and stories from the original *Ties that Bind* still hold true, but some things have changed. I hope to answer some of the most-asked questions I've received and update this book to reflect what networking is like in the digital age. In the end, it still comes down to relationships because we do still need people.

We also need acceptance and social interactions like we need food and shelter. The British psychologist, John Bowlby, observed that newborns and toddlers go to extreme measures to avoid being separated from their caregivers. He developed Attachment Theory, which points out that newborns and toddlers instinctively yearn for this social attachment. Bowlby attributed this to an evolutionary adaptation for survival.[2] In short, we learn almost at birth to cling to each other and seek security through social interaction.

As we grow into adults and build new relationships with friends, co-workers, associates, and romantic partners, our attachment to our parents lessens. While we no longer cling to our parents for safety, we cling to these individuals for the social interaction and relationship security they provide.

We fulfill basic needs through relationships. Some relationships provide satisfaction through close family ties, others through love and intimacy with partners. Still, others find value through relationships with large social groups. Without these relationships, we are left longing for connection, depressed, and alone.

Maslow's Hierarchy of Needs makes clear that after we satisfy our physiological needs (food, water, sleep, etc.) and our safety needs (personal security, financial security, etc.), we strive to fill our love/belonging needs.[3] We need to belong among our social groups. Not everyone has the same desire for acceptance and social interaction, but we all still have these needs on some level.

The primary way this desire for relationships, acceptance, and belonging is achieved in business is through networking. In fact, I often compare the basic steps of networking to dating. I refer to the first meeting with someone as a first date. We ask questions and get to know one another. We try to find out if we are compatible and if the relationship makes sense. The same is true when networking. Follow-up appointments are set, stories and ideas are shared, and trust grows. After a while, business takes place as referrals are passed, and introductions are made. Finally, a trusted business partner becomes a friend, and a real, long-term relationship forms.

This book examines how building a solid network helps fill those basic needs of belonging and acceptance, both professionally and personally. Networking with style is about building solid relationships that allow both parties to benefit. We all have our approaches or styles, and discovering those styles is the best way to make networking comfortable, fun, and ultimately rewarding. A person's network need not be enormous to generate success. Some of the most successful individuals have small but powerful networks. We all benefit from networking once we figure out our styles.

This second edition of *The Ties that Bind: Networking with Style* is divided into three distinct sections centering on themes so that readers can make the most of their time. The first section covers the basics of networking and addresses the fears associated with attending a networking event for the first time. It continues with insight on meeting new people and getting over awkward conversations. I also cover setting reasonable goals and achieving success during and after that first event. It closes with common misunderstandings and fears associated with networking and provides helpful tips and tricks to make the experience more enjoyable.

The second section—Getting More from Your Network —covers how to use the network we all currently have. I explore how becoming conscious of this network is the first step to finding success. Ideas such as "tell people what you want" and "always be helping" show readers how to start using their networks immediately. This section benefits anyone who wants to see better results from their network and to become conscious of the network they already possess.

The final section—Networking with Social Media— provides insight to those curious about using existing social media platforms to expand a personal brand or build a network. This section sees the most significant changes from the first edition as social media has changed so much in the last several years. While the underlying themes and objectives have remained relatively consistent, functionality and user experience have not. The scope of social media is so large that a separate book could be devoted to the subject. For that reason, I offer a high-level overview of three current, popular platforms: Facebook,[4] Twitter, and LinkedIn. We'll also look at networking in the digital age and what it means to connect over software such as Zoom and Teams. I cover strategies to get better results and build a successful online brand. I look at how these platforms are used to connect with individuals face-to-face and build long-lasting, beneficial relationships.

The book does not need to be read in chapter order. Read whatever chapters and topics seem beneficial. Come back to the others at a later time or for a refresher.

Networking does not have to be scary and intimidating. By following the tips and avoiding the pitfalls explained in this book, readers will see the benefits of networking. We all need relationships, and *The Ties that Bind* shows readers how to develop and foster those relationships, all with personal style.

CHAPTER 2

The First Event

Get Out of the Car

The first networking event I attended was a ribbon-cutting for a law firm. I had been in my sales position for over a month, and my trainers recommended I get involved with my local chamber of commerce. It was the first event they hosted after I started my job. As I pulled into a parking spot outside the firm, I felt my pulse quicken and my stomach twist in knots. It got harder to breathe, and I swear the temperature inside my car increased by 10 degrees. I put the car in park and sat there thinking of dozens of reasons not to go in. *Is my hair okay? Am I dressed appropriately? Do I need to be somewhere else? What's for supper? Does my wife need help cleaning the house?* Excuses kept pouring into my head as I tried to open my car door.

Over the next five minutes, I reversed and pulled back into the spot multiple times. I might still be sitting there if not for a stranger who knocked on my passenger window, asking if I was there for the ribbon-cutting. I told him I was, and he offered to go in with me. I finally got out of the car. He introduced himself, we shook hands, and my networking journey began. I am forever indebted to that man. His simple act of kindness was what I needed to take the first step and get out of the car.

Attending your first networking event can be intimidating. Meeting new people, figuring out ways to enter conversations, making small talk, and exiting bad conversations are nerve-racking situations that keep people stuck behind the steering wheel. Surveys show that people fear public speaking more than they fear death; networking is a close second.[5]

The opportunities that networking and building solid relationships provide far outweigh those fears. The easiest way to overcome that fear and get out of the car is to be prepared and have basic strategies in mind.

A quick internet search turns up hundreds of events ranging from business socials to non-profit luncheons to association parties, depending on the size of your community. Narrowing down your focus and determining your goals for attending make getting out of the car easier. Ask yourself some or all of the following questions to narrow your focus and get a better understanding of what you hope to get out of each event:

- Am I attending for business or personal reasons?
- How will I know if attending was a success?
- Does the hosting organization offer additional opportunities for involvement?
- Will future events fit with my personal and professional calendars?
- Do I already know other attendees who will join me?
- Is there someone I can contact prior to attending if I have questions?
- What is the RSVP process?
- What is one objective I want to accomplish to make this event the best use of my time?

These questions narrow your focus and ensure a predetermined measure of success. Setting small goals like meeting one new person or scheduling one follow-up appointment drastically increases the positive use of your time and the odds that you will enjoy the event. These small victories make getting out of the car much less stressful.

The Basics of Networking

Before attending your first or next event, think about the following questions and answer the ones that pertain to your needs.

1. Am I attending for business or personal reasons?

_____

_____

2. How will I know if attending was a success?

_____

_____

_____

_____

_____

3. Will future events fit with my personal and professional calendars?

_____

_____

_____

4. Do I know other attendees who can accompany me? Who?

_____

_____

_____

5. What is one objective I want to accomplish to make this event the best use of my time?

_____

_____

_____

_____

_____

The Buddy System

As I mentioned, there is a good chance I would never have attended that ribbon-cutting without the encouragement of the stranger who knocked on my window. I spent most of the evening talking with and following him as he introduced me to others in attendance. We set an appointment to get coffee the following week, and he offered to attend the next two chamber events with me. I looked forward to seeing my new friend, and at the events, he spent most of his time introducing and connecting me to other professionals. Before long, I no longer felt like I was in a room full of strangers each time I attended a chamber function.

The buddy system—attending an event with a co-worker or friend—is one of the fastest ways to feel more comfortable at a networking event. Having someone you know there can make attending and staying at the event easier, especially if that person is well-connected. I always encourage those new to networking to find someone to accompany them. It is better to attend an event and only talk to one person than never to attend at all.

The other great advantage of bringing a friend is that joint networking can take place. I often challenged coworkers to various contests. Some of these contests included setting up the most follow-up appointments or making the most introductions. In the beginning, we tried a contest to see who could collect the most business cards. We called it "shotgun networking." This method proved a waste of time because we could never connect with people after the event. We each had a desk full of business cards but no relationships. We abandoned this approach even though it was a great tactic to meet a large number of people in a relatively short time.

There is one caveat to using the buddy system: you eventually have to start meeting people on your own. The buddy system is a great way to break the ice, push the comfort zone, and make the first couple of events easier. However, it can be a trap. I have witnessed coworkers attending networking functions and spending the evening huddled in a corner chatting only amongst one another. The same thing happened repeatedly and soon, they stopped attending. A friend of mine, a recruiter, made it to three events in a row with his coworkers. Suddenly he, and everyone he was with, stopped coming. I asked him why. His response: "I wasn't getting anything from them. No business, no new leads; it was a waste of time." It is hard to meet new people when we only talk to those we walk in with.

Know What to Expect

You do your research and find an event that meets your expectations, gives you a chance to meet new people, and allows you to have at least one goal to make attending a success. You put in your RSVP and mark your calendar. Your friend is in the car next to you, and you are ready to walk through the door. So, what should you expect when you attend that first event?

Luckily, most networking events, whether formal or informal, follow a similar program. This structure rings true for 95 percent of the events I've attended:

- Host greeting and nametag area
- Refreshments station
- Open networking for a set amount of time
- Welcome by host
- Program (or ribbon-cutting or speaker)
- Thank you by the host, and a reminder of upcoming events
- Final networking while attendees exit

The host greeting and nametag area are often located near the main entrance. Most organizers have preprinted nametags for those who RSVP'd. This area is also where business cards are dropped for drawings, where additional speaker information is provided, and where registration payments are made. Many organizations have ambassadors whose purpose is to make first-time attendees feel welcome. Take advantage of their kindness. They are typically well-connected and can offer insights as well as be a friendly face at future events.

Also, most events have a refreshments station. The exceptions are luncheons and plated meals. I advise people to show up early if they plan on eating. It is easier to network without food in your mouth or a plate in hand.

Next, the open networking portion is why you are there, so take full advantage. The focus of most events is networking. The fastest way to get over nerves at events is realizing everyone in the room is there for the same reason, to meet new people. Also, keep in mind that they are likely as nervous as you. Use nametags to ask people about their jobs and refer to them by name. As Dale Carnegie famously said in *How to Win Friends and Influence People*, "A person's name is to that person the sweetest and most important sound in any language."[6]

From there, the networking portion ends around 30 to 60 minutes after the start. At this point, the host welcomes everyone in attendance, makes announcements, and turns the stage over to the speaker or begins the formal program. The program should be one of the other reasons you chose to attend. Hopefully, it is something you are interested in or gives you an opportunity to learn something.

As the program ends, the host takes over and thanks everyone for coming. Typically, upcoming events are announced as well as pertinent calls to action such as "be sure to like our Facebook page" or "donations can be made to..." The event officially closes, and people begin to exit. This is the perfect time to make one final connection or collect one last business card. I have the most success setting follow-up appointments during the last five minutes of an event.

Knowing what to expect helps maximize your time and makes navigating the event easier. The hard part is over, as most fear comes from not knowing what to expect.

The next few chapters cover how to best network, such as entering conversations, following standard etiquette, setting valuable appointments, and asking great questions. Now, you must start down the path of meeting new people, expanding your influence, and building a powerful network to make your dreams a reality.

CHAPTER 3

Meeting People

May I Have This Dance?

Think back to middle school and one of the many awkward and embarrassing middle school dances. They were held in a gym or cafeteria. Along one wall were the guys trying to talk about anything to avoid making eye contact with the girls. The girls lined the other wall doing the same thing. In the middle were a handful of brave souls uncomfortably swaying back and forth, a good two feet between them, to a classic slow song.

The night went on. A few more girls made it to the center of the floor in pairs. A couple of guys worked up the courage to say "hi" and ask for a dance. A few more entered the floor, and the process repeated itself. By the end of the evening, most attendees were dancing and completely forgot about that first hour of wall-hugging. The next dance came, and more people started out in the center than on the wall. High school dances got more comfortable. By senior year, no one remembered being the nervous middle school kids who did not want to leave the safety of the wall.

Many first formal networking events are like those first middle school dances. People hang on the outskirts of the room or along the wall watching the regular attendees mingle. Finding the courage to say "hi" and make an introduction can be as terrifying as entering the dance floor for the first time. It gets significantly easier with practice over time.

Here are some things that helped me break the silence and ask people for a dance, networking-wise.

The first thing to remember is, unlike a middle school dance, most people attending a networking event are there for the same reason: to meet new people and make new connections. They want to meet you and do business with you or the people you know. This fact alone makes it easier for me to walk up to strangers and introduce myself at any networking event. The process of wondering if it is OK to introduce myself is simplified when I realize people do want to meet me and hear my story. They want to hear yours, too.

Entering a conversation can be one of the most intimidating parts of the networking process. It is hard to break into a conversation between two or more people when you do not know them. We do not want to come off as rude or abrasive by interrupting the conversation and potentially ruining the chance to make a great new connection. However, we came to network and do not want to stand on the sidelines. There are a few tricks to make getting into conversations less intimidating.

Use the surroundings to your advantage—Depending on the venue or event, it is appropriate, even expected, to talk with others about the function. Fundraising parties and non-profit socials are great because everyone is there for a cause; they want to make a difference or are involved with the charity. Talking about that passion is a great icebreaker. Introduce yourself, and simply ask how the other person is connected with the organization. I have heard some of the most interesting stories and met dynamic people through non-profit functions.

This approach also works at for-profit gatherings, small ribbon-cuttings, and large networking events. It gives the other party the opportunity to lead the conversation and give as much or as little information as they feel comfortable sharing. It is also effective because, in most cases, when the other person finishes telling their story, the individual feels compelled to ask you the same questions. This keeps the conversation moving.

Prepare and find common connections—Some events send the attendee list a week prior to the event. This list is a great tool because it lets everyone see who else will be there. It also gives you the opportunity to find common connections with attendees you want to meet. Use those common connections and ask them to introduce you to others. It's similar to a warm sales lead. It is easier to talk to someone new when a familiar face is right next to you moving the conversation along. Do not be afraid to prepare for two to three introductions to maximize your time.

Wait to be brought in—This can be a hard way to make new connections or enter a conversation because it involves waiting and relying on the kindness of others, but it works extraordinarily well. The tactic is simple. Stand on the fringe of a group of individuals you want to meet. Listen to the conversation, make eye contact with the speakers, and wait. It takes a lull in the conversation or until someone brings you into the group, but waiting is worth it. Once you have been brought into the conversation, you will be introduced to everyone in the group and are usually given center stage to talk about what you do, who you are, or why you are at the event. In my experience, it is the fastest way to meet a large group of people. You can also use a combination of preparation and waiting to be brought in.

Most events do not provide a list of attendees. Instead of planning ahead, I look around an event for a familiar face in a group of people I may not know. I stand on the fringe next to the person I know and wait to be brought into the conversation by them. It speeds up the waiting and, again, provides a warm introduction to the rest of the group. It also goes faster because the person I know does a short introduction for me, so the group will know my name and what I do before I open my mouth.

Flattery can get you everywhere—The wonderful thing about most events—whether non-profit, for-profit, casual, or structured—is the people. I have met individuals new to their careers all the way up to CEOs. The common thread they all appreciate is honest, heartfelt praise. Imagine someone coming up to you, shaking your hand, introducing himself, and then sharing how he wanted to meet you because of the amazing things you do professionally. He shares stories he has heard about your success and how much he admires what you do for the community. Some may feel embarrassed by this praise. Others may feel proud that their accomplishments are recognized. The majority will be more than willing to talk to a newfound admirer because that admirer demonstrated genuine interest.

Genuine praise, compliments, or flattery, whatever it is called, all work because they show the new connection that you took the time to learn more about who they are and what they do. We all love to be admired and meet people who want to learn more about us. They also make getting into the conversation easier because the first talking point is prede-termined and leaves the other person feeling good from the outset.

Be someone's hero—Look around the room and find someone who is hanging on the outskirts, hugging the wall, or looking nervous and alone. There is someone like this at almost every event. It may be that person's first event, the person may be new to the job and trying this out for the first time, or the person may be new to town and wanting to meet people. Whatever the case, that person desperately wants someone to talk to and to make them feel welcome. Be the hero and say "hi."

This was one way I began building my network when I was new. I looked around the room and often saw small groups talking and laughing like old friends. I was intimidated and did not know how to insert myself into those conversations. Instead, I would look around and try to find someone who looked as nervous as I felt. Some of my best and longest-lasting relationships came from walking up to someone who felt alone in a room full of people. A simple hello and friendly conversation can make someone's day and turn around an uncomfortable experience.

Ask Better Questions

The final tip is this: Do not overthink the introductory conversation. All we are doing is asking for that first dance. A smile and a handshake are still common practices and a great way to break the ice. I like to introduce myself and then have one or two conversation starters in mind. They are great because they keep conversations moving and prevent the dreaded awkward silence. They keep the dance swaying back and forth. Some typical conversation starters include:

- Talking about the event space or location
- Asking why they're attending the event and what they hope to get out of it
- Asking "Where are you from?" or "Where did you go to school?"

- Asking "What are you passionate about?" or "What do you do for fun?"
- My personal favorite is "What's your story?"

This may come as a shock, but I will generally avoid talking about work as much as possible when meeting someone new. None of the questions above ask about work or what someone does for a living, and this is by design. Right Management, a subsidiary of Manpower, found that only 19 percent of workers are satisfied in their jobs, according to a survey from June of 2012.[7] Year after year, articles are put out by Inc. magazine, Entrepreneur.com, *The Wall Street Journal*, and more, explaining that roughly 67% or two-thirds of the population don't like what they do for a living. This number can vary slightly from year to year, but it's almost always the same. Imagine starting a conversation with a new acquaintance and immediately asking them to talk about something they hate. When you ask someone what they do for a living, this is essentially what you're doing for two-thirds of the people you meet. I do not want to start a conversation with a new connection by asking them about something they do not enjoy.

Each of the other questions allows for finding common ground. It is much easier to strengthen a new connection that way. By talking about the event space or featured group, we can discover common interests. Inquiring about where the person grew up or went to school allows us to discover mutual connections. Numerous times, I have met someone who attended my alma mater, which led to discussions about professors, cafeteria food, homecoming, and traditions. Occasionally, we discover we lived in the same dorm building or knew the same people.

The question "What are you passionate about?" or the less aggressive "What do you do for fun?" delivers the most unique answers and helps cement a new relationship. They allow the connection to talk about whatever they want to share without leading the conversation. I love it because it allows me to quickly discover what other people enjoy doing. If they truly love their jobs, they will discuss their jobs. If they love their families, they will share those stories. If they have hobbies, favorite non-profits, or unique experiences, these questions allow them to share those details.

True gold can be found with the final question, "What's your story?" This is the most open-ended question and truly allows for the other person to determine where they want the conversation to go. They can talk about where they grew up, what they loved early in life, what they did after graduation, their family, their hobbies, their career aspirations, and whatever they want without limitations. Some of the most interesting conversations I've had were directly related to asking this simple question. I have learned about things ranging from archery to cross stitch simply because I did not ask about work. The conversations have been more genuine as well.

It also opens the door for the new connection to reciprocate. This allows me to build on what we have in common. It also allows for the relationship to deepen, as the give and take of the conversation enlightens each party about the other. The next time you meet someone, try using one of these conversation starters. You may be surprised how quickly it can turn an awkward situation into an enjoyable experience for both parties.

Ask Better Questions

Meeting new people and talking with strangers can be very intimidating. Answer the following conversation starters so you don't get put on the spot. Be sure to use these questions when meeting someone for the first time.

1. Why are you attending the event? (Be specific. If it's a charity event, talk about your involvement with the charity; if it's a business function, talk about what you do and what you're trying to accomplish.)

_____

_____

_____

_____

_____

_____

2. What's your story?

_____

_____

_____

_____

_____

3. What are you passionate about, or what do you do for fun?

_____

_____

_____

_____

Can I Get Your Number?

Believe it or not, in this age of smartphones, social media, and hundreds of apps, the business card is alive and well.[8] It is still a universally accepted tool that allows for quick information sharing with little to no pressure. I typically use the business card to get contact information into my database or connect with the individual on LinkedIn. Without it, this task would be much harder. The business card is succinct, simple, and allows for a quick exchange of information.

Dozens of articles from influencers in various industries explain how they no longer carry business cards because they rely on the new connection to have one. They will ask for a card and then email relevant contact information. I have been guilty of this when I forget to bring cards to an event. I do not like this approach because there have been countless instances when those I've met did not have cards. I gave them my card and asked for emails with contact information. The emails never came. A few weeks would go by, and I would see them again and ask about getting that email. Time and time again, I experienced the same reaction: a sheepish smile followed by an apology for forgetting. "I've been so busy. I must have forgotten."

Another issue with this approach is that fewer cards will be available as more and more adopt it. The fact is we are all busy. Why leave it up to chance that the new connection will send that promised email? Why not have a card to ensure follow-up calls or meetings happen without relying on the other person? The business card is an inexpensive extension of your personal branding.

I still give out business cards without receiving them all the time. They may end up in the trash, but they also may result in a great appointment. One example: I entered a CPA's office one afternoon during a busy day of cold calling. The CPA was working on tax returns for customers who filed extensions earlier in the year. I apologized for bothering him while he was busy. He smiled and said he appreciated the break. We talked briefly about how his business was going, and I gave him a quick overview of the company I was working for. Five minutes went by, and he said he better get back to work. I thanked him for his time, gave him my card, and left the building. Two weeks later, my phone rang. It was the same CPA who was calling to refer a client to me. Since that time, he has given me dozens of referrals, resulting in hundreds of thousands of dollars of new business. He had no other way to contact me besides my business card, and I never received his contact information until we worked on the first client together. Imagine the outcome had I not been carrying business cards that day.

When a conversation with a new contact ends, do not be afraid to ask for a business card. It is an expected question at networking functions. Always pass yours whether the new connection has one or not. When the other person does not have a card, I will ask for a phone number or email address and write it on the back of my card. I also ask if they are on LinkedIn.

Sometimes, it is appropriate to send the new connection an email or text to exchange contact information. We have so many ways to communicate now that it may require adapting to the new connection's preferred form of communication, such as emails, Facebook Messenger, Snapchat, text messages, phone calls, face-to-face meetings, and countless others. Discover how the new connection prefers to communicate by simply asking. Using the preferred method provides a better chance of connecting outside the event.

It all comes down to making sure you collect some way to follow up after the event. A business card is the easiest way to achieve this. As times change and we rely more on digital communication, be willing to adapt and offer to connect through other means. Most importantly, get the other person's information, and be sure to use it.

To Eat or Not to Eat

Most networking events have food and beverages ranging from cheese and vegetable trays to heavy hors d'oeuvres. Beverages could include water, soda, wine, and beer. It is the intention of the host for guests to enjoy these refreshments. They can be enticing and delicious. They can also be disastrous if not given proper respect.

I once attended an event with a full bar and large spread

of some of the best food I ever experienced while networking. I did my research and knew influential individuals would be attending. They had not yet arrived, so I piled up my appetizer plate with shrimp, meatballs, hummus, and more. It was delicious, and I made sure to compliment the host on her taste. Everything was going well until I bumped into the back of someone, and a meatball rolled off my plate and down the center of my white shirt. There is not a stain stick large enough to undo that damage. Needless to say, I did not meet the people I had hoped, as I hurriedly left to change.

Another incident happened shortly after that. A friend and I were attending an after-work social. We left the office early so that we could arrive at the event 15 minutes before it was scheduled to begin. Each of us grabbed a beer and made our way around the room. He grabbed a plate of food and was standing in the corner when a lady walked up to him and introduced herself. He fumbled with the plate, trying to find a place to set it down, and as he was bending down to put it on a nearby ledge, he tipped his beer down the front of her blouse. I had never seen that particular shade of red on a person's face before as he apologized again and again. She was calm as she tried to sop up the beer. They both left shortly after, him out of embarrassment and her to change clothes.

Food and drink are typically a highlight, and the host has spent time and money to provide it, so it would be rude not to partake. But navigating a room, meeting new people, and enjoying refreshments can be tricky. The best piece of advice I received on managing this is to arrive early. Arriving early, even five minutes, allows you to enjoy refreshments without the worry of making small talk with a mouth full of food or where to put plates and cups to shake hands.

Another way to save the hassle of figuring out what to do with a cup or plate is to only partake of one or the other at any given time. This allows for an open hand for greetings and makes it easier to navigate the room. Always keep one hand free; you never know when you will need it.

The final pointer is to enjoy in moderation. No one likes the person who has one drink too many or has an overflowing plate of food. The refreshments provided are meant to be enjoyed, so enjoy them. However, know your limits and the potential impact of excess on your first impression.

Please, Stop Talking

Over the years, I have found myself stuck in conversations. The initial pleasantries have been exchanged, and, for one reason or another, the conversation should be over, but it is not. The other person keeps talking, sharing details, or hovering long enough that an extended silence cannot be used to excuse yourself from the conversation. Those new to networking may not have experienced this yet. Others are nodding in agreement.

As a rule, I try to find something interesting in every person I meet. We all have stories, quirks, and things that make us unique and fun. However, there are times when the conversation gets awkward or goes on too long. A way out is needed. Here is what works for me.

Use drinks to your advantage. Drinks need refilling.

When I find myself in an unproductive conversation, I excuse myself to refill my drink. This allows me to leave the conversation without offending the other party.

Introduce a useful connection. As conversations progress and reach natural endings, introducing a useful connection or friend is an easy transition. I am not recommending putting a friend in a situation you are not enjoying; I am suggesting only to introduce someone if it makes sense for both parties to meet. For example, I might introduce a mortgage banker to a real estate agent I was talking to if the conversation was winding down, but we couldn't figure out how to end it.

When in doubt, ask for a business card. A business card is the universal signal that the conversation is finished. The trick is to ask for a card before offering yours. Tell the person you enjoyed the conversation and would like to follow up. Then, politely ask for a card. Typically, you will be asked for yours in return. Do not worry if you do not have one because you already have the new contact's information. A quick handshake, a smile, and a thank you later, and the conversation is over.

Do them the favor of ending the conversation. This is my favorite. When a conversation is coming to a close, I use the following dialog:

"It was so nice to meet you this evening. I do not want to monopolize your time tonight, and I know you want to make other connections. Let's connect later. Thank you so much for your time. Good luck networking!"

This allows the other person to feel good about the conversation ending on a high note.

The purpose is always to make the end of the conversation as positive as possible. This way, the relationship can continue, and the opportunity for future conversations remains strong. Leave the other party feeling good, and make sure to follow up when the conversation can be used to build a long-term relationship.

CHAPTER 4

Now What?

The Art of the Follow-Up:
I Want a Cup of Coffee, Not a Date

There is no point in networking without follow-up. It is the most important part of the process, and it is something most of us mess up. Despite my earlier comparison, I want to be absolutely clear: networking is not dating. There is no 24- or 48-hour rule, no guideline about who should call first, and no risk of sounding desperate with an immediate meeting request. In short, networking is about getting things done.

The only way to do that is to follow up.

I try to set at least one follow-up meeting during each networking event. All of us carry our calendars in our pockets through smartphones, which makes it easy to set appointments, so ask. Explain that you enjoyed getting to know the person and ask if they would be willing to meet in the following days or weeks. If this is not your style, do not be afraid to email the person as soon as you get back to your office. Often, this is easier with people you just met because you are fresh on their minds.

The final piece is persistence. Do not give up after one email or one voicemail. Multiple times, I've had to email or call a person a dozen times to set an appointment. When I finally got the person on the phone, I apologized for leaving so many messages. Their responses often surprise me: "No need to apologize. I kept meaning to call you back, but things kept coming up." They often thank me for my persistence.

Getting good at following up does not take an overly complicated calendar or call strategy. It takes persistence and a desire to connect. Remember: without a good follow-up plan, there is no point in attending networking events.

The Follow-Up

Networking is not dating, and there is no follow-up rule. Make it a priority to meet one interesting person you can have a meeting with outside of the event to get to know better.

1. Who did I meet that I want to follow up with after the event? (Name, Email, Phone)

_____

_____

_____

_____

_____

_____

2. What will we talk about in our meeting? (Examples: What do you do for fun? Where are you from? What do you do in your free time? Where did you go to school? What's your biggest dream? What do you like most about your job?)

_____

_____

_____

_____

_____

_____

3. Following the meeting, ask yourself if it was successful. Why or why not?

_____

_____

_____

_____

_____

Judging Success

The event is over, business cards are filed, connections are made, and appointments are set. Was the event successful? Was it a good use of your valuable time? It depends on how you define success. In networking, success depends on previous experience, individual expectations, or personal and professional goals. The way I define networking success changed drastically from when I started.

Compared to today, I had completely different expectations for my first networking event, the ribbon-cutting at the law firm I mentioned earlier. My goal was to meet as many people as possible and sell my services, hopefully to the law firm's owners. I met one of those goals by meeting a great group of individuals. The other was not realistic. I realized over time that most people were not going to buy my services after the initial meeting. That would take persistence and time.

The success of networking requires our most valuable resource: time. The better we use our time and set realistic expectations, the better our chances of success. I strongly advise those new to networking to evaluate what they want to achieve and pick organizations or events to attend based on those goals. Find an area where success is possible, and there is a higher probability you will stick with it through to the end.

The same goes for realistic goals based on your personality and job requirements. Salespeople have different goals than those in marketing or non-profit work. Make sure you understand what those requirements are beforehand and make it a priority to see that the event you attend fulfills your requirements.

The interesting person rule is the simplest barometer for judging whether an event was successful and a good use of your time. I make it a priority to meet at least one new and interesting person at each event. By meeting at least one person with whom I can have a genuine conversation, I expand my network and, ultimately, my influence. The great part about this rule is that the first new person I meet usually fulfills this requirement.

Before heading out, ask yourself these questions, which should help clarify your expectations and guarantee your success.

- What one thing do I want this event to accomplish?
- Will this event allow me to accomplish this goal?
- Is there something I could do that is more productive or will yield better results?
- How many people do I want to meet?
- What is my follow-up strategy?

Set clear expectations before you attend the event, and stick to those goals. This creates success and gives you instant gratification that you can, in fact, achieve success through networking. Like all things worth doing in life, networking takes time, but achieving even minor success makes it easier to keep coming back.

Judging Success

Fill out the following questions after attending the first event to see if it was successful.

1. Did I accomplish my goal, and what did I learn? (Met one new person, had a good conversation, got over a fear)

_____

_____

_____

_____

_____

2. What is my follow-up strategy moving forward?

_____

_____

_____

_____

_____

_____

3. Was this event a good use of my time, and will I attend another function put on by the same organization? Why or why not?

_____

_____

_____

_____

Run the Networking Race

In 2012, I completed the Des Moines Marathon. My goal for that race was not to come in first or finish in the top 50 percent. It was simply to finish. The race itself was brutal and exhausting, but I would never have finished without training. Those preceding 12 weeks of running conditioned and toned my muscles and cardiovascular system and enabled me to complete the race. I was willing to put in the time to achieve the result.

There are similarities between completing a marathon and building a solid network. First, both take time. People continually tell stories about how networking does not work for them. When I ask how long they have networked, I hear anything from a few weeks to a few months. Most people want instant gratification, and when they do not see a return immediately, they give up. A good network takes time to build. New connections need time to develop trust, just like legs need time to adjust to long-distance running.

Second, both activities require effort and follow-through. Around the sixth week of marathon training, I was ready to give up. The miles piled up, and my body was breaking down. The same can be said for building a network. Numerous times, I don't feel like attending an event or meeting new people. It is OK to take a day off now and again, as long as it stays at a day or two. Relationships need to be fostered to grow, and that can only be accomplished through effort and follow-through by both parties.

Finally, both marathons and good networks start with that

first step. No one completed a race from the couch, just like no one built a network sitting in a car. That first step need not be a 10k or an event with 300-plus people. It is OK to start small and go a lap around the block as long as you are giving yourself the opportunity. Someone once said, "No matter how slow you go, you're still lapping everyone on the couch." I believe that holds true whether you are running or networking.

Remember, networking takes time; it takes time to build real relationships and earn people's trust.

CHAPTER 5

Become Conscious

The next section of this book covers building relationships once the event concludes. We will discover how to get the most from our current networks and ways to make both our personal and professional dreams a reality through networking.

We Are All Networking, All the Time

I made a major career change in 2008 and accepted a position with CitiMortage. My previous job was a dead end. In hindsight, moving to a mortgage company in 2008 was not the best decision I ever made. The mortgage industry fell apart, and I was handed a pink slip when the company closed its Des Moines operations. That was one of the worst nights of my life. I remember telling my wife and seeing the tears well up in her eyes. She asked the same question I had repeated in my head all day: "What are we going to do?"

I vowed never to be in that situation again. I never wanted to tell my wife I was unemployed or to listen to her quietly sob next to me in bed. It was terrifying. I had no one to turn to. I could not make a phone call and find a job because I did not know enough people in the area. I spent the following weeks on countless other job sites. I sent out hundreds of resumes, made follow-up calls, and eventually landed a job in sales.

During the first week of sales training, my mentor told me point blank, "The first year of sales is going to be hard. You are going to have to cold call, pound the pavement, and start meeting people. You also have to start building a referral network immediately." I took those words to heart and began attending chamber meetings and networking groups and started volunteering with non-profits. Eventually, I amassed a network of individuals working with me to create business. It did not happen overnight, but the time I put in was well worth it. I was successfully networking.

This newly established network did great things for my career, and it began to trickle into my personal life. I found myself hanging out with my new connections on weekends and meeting their families. We became more than business associates; we became friends. Our kids played together, and we celebrated each other's birthdays. We wanted to help each other succeed outside of what we did for a living. What started as a way to help me hit my sales numbers transformed into something bigger.

The biggest epiphany I had was when I realized everyone is networking all the time. When you make small talk with a cashier at a grocery store, you are networking. Going to the mall or seeing a movie with friends is networking. Posting on Facebook, sending a tweet, and linking or sharing on Instagram are all networking. Once we become aware that networking is taking place all around us, we can take advantage of the opportunities. As soon as you become conscious of the network you have, you can capitalize on your connections.

The second test of my network came in May of 2018. The company that I had spent the better part of a decade working for sold to a competitor, and I quickly found myself in a new culture that wasn't the right fit. Many years prior, a Central College alumnus named Dennis Markway had approached me at a networking event we were both attending on campus. He told me he wanted to hire me someday as we were shaking hands. I remember his boldness catching me off guard, but I took his card and kept his offer in the back of my mind. He was the first call I made when I came to the realization that I needed to make a change.

Dennis is the owner of Iron Horse Wealth Management, LLC in Johnston, Iowa. As we discussed his offer and the opportunity for me to join his firm as a financial advisor, I remember thinking, "Well, I hope everything I wrote about in my book wasn't crap because I'm about to start over." I re-read *The Ties that Bind* just before I started working for Dennis. It was a good reminder of strategies I had either forgotten or had simply stopped using as my career had accelerated. I started attending events and having coffee with anyone who would listen to my story and wanted to connect.

It turns out my book wasn't crap. Each new goal and metric I set for myself was achieved in large part through my networking. People happily connected to hear about my career change and simply catch up. Business started to come in, and so did referrals. A couple short years later I became a partner at Iron Horse, and I have my network to thank.

Create the Chance to Connect

A close friend had coffee with Suku Radia, who was the CEO of the largest locally-owned bank in Iowa. During the meeting, my friend inquired about why Radia agreed to meet him. After all, my friend was new to the working world, had little to no clout, and did not have much to offer. Radia smiled, "The first meeting is free. You have to earn the second." The CEO of a billion-dollar enterprise would meet with anyone once. The implication of those words changed my life because if he could give anyone one meeting, then I should be able to do the same.

I also realized I did not have to hesitate to ask people to connect. Up to that point, I had confidence issues when reaching out to certain individuals because their titles or influence intimidated me. My lack of confidence held me back. Now, "The first meeting is free. You have to earn the second," is what I hear when I send an email or make a phone call that causes my confidence to falter. Surprisingly, I have been told no far fewer times than yes.

Since hearing that story, I've had hundreds of meetings with individuals ranging from those fresh out of college to executive directors of non-profits to CEOs of international companies. I have yet to turn down a meeting request even when I knew the person had no other intentions than to sell me something. Everyone has a story, and everyone has something of value to offer, even if they do not realize it. Our jobs are to find that value.

One such meeting occurred almost by accident. I started a new job, and two weeks in, the person who hired me gave her two-week notice and moved halfway across the United States. She put together a list of interesting people I should reach out to before she left. On that list was a man named Steve Chapman. She circled his photograph and wrote, "You must meet him. He will change your life." Under his picture were an email address and phone number. I sent him an email and went back to work.

A few weeks later, Chapman emailed letting me know he was available the following week. We agreed on a time and place. I confess I did no research before I met him. The morning of our meeting came, and I casually strolled into the coffee shop in a suit with no tie. There sat Chapman in a professional suit with a red tie. I felt sheepish as I sat down and apologized for being underdressed. He smiled and told me not to worry.

I continued to apologize that I had done no research on

him. I explained that my former boss told me I had to meet him because she said he would change my life. He smiled and said to pass on his thanks to my boss. Then I asked who he was and if he could tell me his story. Over the next 90 minutes, I sat in silence as he told me about his former position as CEO of ITA Group in West Des Moines. He explained how he was currently serving as CEO of Ruan, one of Des Moines' largest corporations. He described how he came in during the recession to help the company through challenging times. He talked about his philanthropic work and mentioned some of the honors the community bestowed on him.

My former boss was right. The end of that meeting came, and I felt like a better person for having the opportunity to talk with Chapman. He made me feel like I mattered just as much as his closest friend, even though I did not know anything about him before I walked into that coffee shop. He even lined up meetings for me with other prominent community leaders. None of this would have happened without my former boss or the email she told me to send.

Give people the opportunity to meet you and create connections. The worst anyone can say is no. Do not be afraid to ask for meetings to build relationships and expand your network. Always remember: "The first meeting is free. You have to earn the second."

Try Something New

It is incredibly easy to become stagnant at networking. It is easy to attend the same functions put on by the same organizations and shake the same hands month after month and year after year. We become comfortable because we know most of the people in the room. The conversations are easy. The anxiety of meeting new people has worn off. Do not fall into this trap.

I attend at least one new event each quarter where I may know only one or two of the attendees. This forces me to be on my toes. It also ensures that I will continue to meet individuals who may add value to my existing network. By attending new events and meeting new people, I never get complacent.

New events are not hard to find. There are hundreds of organizations putting on networking events. It takes a little effort to find a new function, but sometimes it can present itself as a recommendation from a good friend. For me, one such opportunity came when a close friend was going through a leadership program. He invited me to the kickoff party for their class project: a massive fundraiser to help a local non-profit with its capital campaign.

Throughout the night, I met many individuals of various backgrounds who were in completely different circles from my own. Toward the end of the evening, I was introduced to the executive director of the non-profit. We hit it off and scheduled coffee the following week. During our coffee, she asked if I would serve on the non-profit's advisory committee. I jumped at the opportunity.

The appointment to the advisory committee for Amanda the Panda allowed me to help individuals in my community who are grieving the loss of loved ones. This organization touches so many people and helps them through the hardest times of their lives. It also allowed me to connect with a whole new group of individuals and build friendships with people I would have never met if not for that event.

Do not become complacent. Meet new people and get out of your comfort zone. Find a new event or sample what another group is doing. This allows you to grow your network, expand your influence, and become involved in rewarding opportunities.

Look Up

Distractions are everywhere. We have smartphones, tablets, social media, phone calls, text messages, emails, and so on. It is easy to connect with people all over the planet. We can answer almost any question that comes to mind through a quick Google search. It is so bad in the U.S. that people send or receive at least 35 texts per day, and 28 percent of the average office worker's time is spent on email.[9] Look around the park, mall, office, or your home, and you will see people looking at digital devices.

Look Up, a YouTube video posted in 2014 by Gary Turk, is a five-minute, narrated film that shows the downside of our reliance on technology and devices. Turk follows the imaginary life of a man who meets the love of his life when he gets lost on a city street. He has a piece of paper in his hand with an address and, after realizing he has lost his way, asks a stranger for help. She turns out to be his soul mate, and the video walks through the life they build together. However, this never happens. The man never got lost because he had a smartphone and used GPS. As Turk laments, "When you're too busy looking down, you don't see the chances you miss."[10] The same thing happens in most social settings. I have seen people checking their phones during lunch meetings, networking events, and prospecting calls. I have been guilty of it in the past and will be guilty of it in the future. Our phones provide a level of comfort and, as research is finding,[11] can be as addictive as drugs because of the dopamine released each time we experience a positive interaction on our devices.

The distraction of a phone or any other device is a huge hindrance when building a new relationship or meeting new people. It causes broken eye contact, missed conversation points, and poor listening. It sends the message to the new connection that they are not as important as whatever is on our phones. At its least, it is distracting. At its worst, it is rude and can lead to the loss of a new connection before it begins.

The expression "You only get one chance to make a first impression" is still true. The fastest way to destroy that impression is to check your phone when someone else is trying to connect. The easiest way to combat this constant distraction is to remember to be in the moment when meeting a new person. Treat them like they are the only person in the room and put all distractions aside. Make good eye contact with them and actively listen to whatever story they tell. Ask follow-up questions and probe for understanding. That email, text, or snap will be there later, but the person you are talking to may not. Look up and give the other person the respect and attention they deserve.

CHAPTER 6

CREATE REAL CONNECTIONS

Find Their Stories First

I had the opportunity to go through the Dale Carnegie course when I was working at Hy-Vee. Until that class, I always found it difficult to engage with strangers and make small talk. In fact, I hated it. Discussing the weather or the latest news seemed shallow. The best lesson I learned from that course was that everyone has a story; everyone has something interesting that makes them open up and want to share. The easiest way to connect with people is to find that story.

This fits with the earlier section about asking better questions. By asking a person what they are passionate about or what they do for fun, we actively look for that story. What may seem like small talk is actually searching for the thing that makes a person unique. It may not happen the first time we ask, but as time goes on and trust builds, this question will be answered, and a new level of relationship develops. The next step in finding a story is to listen and actively engage in whatever turns the conversation takes. Once someone starts opening up and telling their story, they must become the most important person in the room, no matter who walks in the door or what else happens. It is only by making that person the center of attention that you engage in the conversation and ask the questions that continue the story. By listening and inquiring for more information or deeper meaning, we continue the story and give the person more opportunities to shine. It is finding that story that makes someone a great conversationalist.

Before you continue reading, put this book down for a couple of minutes and think about your story. What is the one story you could repeatedly tell if someone would listen? Maybe it was running a marathon, a great vacation, a book that brought you to tears, watching your first child being born, or starting your first business. Think about the last time you told that story and how it made you feel. Now imagine giving someone else the opportunity to tell a story that made them feel the same way. A great story can build relationships and strengthen bonds. It is up to you to find that story if you want to build a successful, reliable network.

Getting More from Your Network

What is your story? Having an engaging story is a great way to find commonalities and make connections outside of the typical business small talk. Take a moment to create your unique story. Think about things such as:

• What do I love to do in my free time?

• What makes me unique?

• What could I talk about for hours if given the opportunity?

• Do I have a hobby or interest that others might find interesting?

• What is my proudest accomplishment?

What is your story? Write it below:

_____

_____

_____

_____

_____

_____

_____

_____

_____

_____

_____

_____

_____

_____

_____

_____

_____

_____

_____

_____

_____

_____

_____

_____

_____

_____

The Rule of Reciprocation

In November of 2012, I heard an interesting story on NPR's Morning Edition about the rule of reciprocation. It told how Phillip Kunz, a sociologist at Brigham Young University, sent 600 Christmas cards to complete strangers in 1974. Over the following weeks, he received more than 200 cards back from these strangers because of the basic human desire to reciprocate.

What does this have to do with networking and building relationships? Everything. The NPR story explained one of my favorite points: "If someone passes you in the hall and says hello, you feel compelled to return their greeting. When you don't, you notice it, [sic] it makes you uncomfortable, out of balance. That's the rule of reciprocation."[12] It is the same reason conversations work. The give and take, the disclosing and expecting disclosure help the ebb and flow of conversation.

We ask others to share their stories and what they do for fun, both to learn about that person and to have the opportunity to share our stories. The rule of reciprocation dictates that once they have shared their stories, they will feel compelled to ask you about yours. They want to return the favor or repay kindness with kindness. By allowing them to share their stories, by listening intently, and by asking good questions, you open the door for them to do the same.

I cannot guarantee this is the case with 100 percent of conversations, but it happens in the majority. This is the reason you need a good story. That story should be in your head already, but if it is not, review the questions on the previous guided worksheet and take the time to write some answers. You may be surprised by how interesting you are!

Now that you've developed a story you can share with enthusiasm and passion, one that makes you excited and shows who you are, run this story through your mind a few times before your next meeting or networking event. Work out the details ahead of time, so when the opportunity comes, you can share it and share it well. I am not recommending memorizing it or practicing it to the point that it becomes a rehearsed, robotic speech. I am recommending that you prepare so that when the opportunity arises, and you are asked about your passions, you can shine.

It's Not What You Know...

The phrase "It's not what you know; it's who you know" cannot be attributed to any one individual. My favorite story on the origin of the saying is from a *NY Tribune* article that dates it to 1918 when shipyard workers along the Delaware River adopted it as a war slogan.[13] The workers went on strike after the shipyard hired several non-skilled laborers, such as baseball players who were forced out of non-essential jobs for wartime efforts. These laborers were hired not for their abilities but because they knew the right people. To make matters worse, they did the least amount of work possible to remain employed, thus the strike. The saying is as valuable now as it was in 1918.

It is so easy in today's environment of constant communication to get in contact with just about anyone. Countless social media platforms have given us the opportunity to connect with people across the globe with nothing more than the click of a mouse. We accept friends on Facebook, connect on LinkedIn, and follow on Twitter often with the hopes of expanding our networks and building real-life relationships. Many times, these tactics fail. We are so busy running our personal and professional lives that, sometimes, it is easier to ignore those requests and continue our routines. This is why the personal introduction is such a powerful way to help people connect and to build your network.

I have yet to have a trusted connection turn down an introduction I made, and I have never personally turned down an introduction someone made to me. The wonderful thing about introductions is that the person being introduced has already been vetted and passed someone else's tests. There is no worry about whether the meeting will be a success because a trusted friend is making the recommendation.

One of my closest friends, Kim Gratny, is a master at this. We met over cinnamon rolls at the Machine Shed in early 2015. She had seen an article I had written for the *Business Record*, a Des Moines area business magazine, on making new connections for the New Year. The article caught her attention, so she reached out to learn more. We hit it off immediately.

Toward the end of the breakfast, she asked if there was anything she could help me with. I smiled and told her that if she knew anyone I should connect with, to simply do the introduction. They didn't need to be a business prospect; they just needed to be someone she genuinely thought I would enjoy meeting. I also told her she didn't need to ask my permission, just send the intro email, and I would have the meeting because I trusted her judgment. She smiled and asked if I would be willing to do the same for her.

Over the next several years, Kim has sent me dozens of unsolicited connections. Simple emails giving me and my new acquaintance some background information on one another and the reason for the introduction. I have taken her up on all of these connections without question because I want to make myself open to new opportunities and relationships. Some have turned into friendships, and others were simply good "get to know you" meetings. I have learned something from everyone she has connected me with.

The craziest meeting happened shortly after I started my new career at Iron Horse. Kim sent an intro email that read like most of her others. It was an intro to a friend she had who was looking to get more from her existing network, and she thought I could be a good resource for her. I scheduled the coffee and didn't even take the time to Google who I was meeting with. I trusted Kim and wanted to go into the meeting with no preconceived expectations.

My new connection and I talked about her career and why she was looking to activate her network. It turned out she had recently become the CEO of a marketing company in Des Moines after buying out the previous owner. We spoke about possible connections and what markets she wanted to get into. As the coffee came to a close, she asked me what I did. I explained that I was a financial advisor and worked with companies on their retirement plans. She paused for a second and remarked that she hadn't heard from her plan's advisor since she had taken over the company. She then asked if I would be willing to look over her plan and provide any feedback I could.

A few short weeks later, we were doing paperwork to move the plan to me as the advisor, and I moved one step closer to my goal of becoming a partner within the firm. I asked Kim later if she knew that this opportunity existed, and she confessed that she did not. She simply thought that it would be a good idea for me and the CEO to know one another. Had I not taken the meeting or blown it off because I was too "busy" with other things, I would have missed this incredible opportunity.

Make yourself available to give and receive introductions whenever possible. Always be willing to introduce trusted connections if it will make a difference personally or professionally. Ask connections for introductions and be willing to return the favor. A great introduction builds business, develops new relationships, helps reach goals, and makes a direct and immediate impact on people's lives. Help create those introductions and watch your own network and influence grow. After all, it's not what you know; it's who you know.

Tell People What You Want

I graduated from the West Des Moines Leadership Academy in the summer of 2012. During our graduation ceremony, we brought in Mitch Matthews, the creator of the Big Dream Gathering and a wonderful speaker on taking action on dreams. He walked the class through an exercise where we wrote down our dreams, no matter how outlandish, on pieces of paper and hung those papers throughout the room. I decided to make one of my hidden dreams known; I wanted to start public speaking. I wrote the dream on my paper and hung it on the wall hoping someone would help.

The next part of the exercise consisted of each class member walking around the room and reading each other's dreams. We were instructed to leave contact information or advice if we could help our classmates achieve a dream. As the session concluded, we gathered our dreams off the wall, shook hands, and parted as graduates and friends. I rushed to my dream sheet about becoming a speaker and received a minor shock. There was Mitch's number with the brief note, "Call me; I'd love to help." I glanced around the room and made eye contact with Mitch. He smiled and did the "call me" signal.

The next afternoon, I called him and set up a coffee. We met, and I explained my dream in more detail: I wanted to speak about networking to small businesses and colleges because I felt my message heavily impacted those groups. I had never heard of or tried to network in college or in my first few jobs. My life would be completely different if I had only known the power of networking earlier. I wanted to share that message.

We talked for over an hour, and when we finished, I had a basic roadmap of my speaking career in front of me. I took his advice to heart, and a few short months later, I landed my first presentation. Another month went by, and I booked my first paid engagement. Since that coffee, I have made thousands of dollars speaking and have at least one presentation each month with as many as four to five per month. This happened because I shared my dream.

This brings me to the essential lesson of this book. The fastest and most efficient way to get your network working for you is to tell people what you want.

Do not hold back. Tell anyone who will listen what you want to accomplish and let them know how they can help. Give specific goals and dreams. Do not be afraid to ask for help. The worst anyone can say is no.

My wife became a believer in this philosophy in 2011.

We are both huge Iowa State fans. During the 2011 season, they won enough games to become eligible for a bowl game. We sat in eager anticipation, waiting to see where they would play. At one point, I poked her with my elbow and suggested we go to the game if they made the Pinstripe Bowl in New York City. It would be played the day before New Year's Eve, so we could go to the game and be in Times Square for the ball drop. She smiled and immediately agreed. A few minutes later, the announcement came. Iowa State would play in the Pinstripe Bowl.

She let out a yelp, and I ran to the computer to book a flight and get game tickets. I started looking for a hotel room, and my stomach sank. There was little availability because it was already close to New Year's Eve. The rooms that were available were insanely over our budget. We sat down dejected and wondered what to do. Suddenly, my wife pulled out her computer and typed a post on Facebook: "My husband and I are going to NYC for the Pinstripe Bowl and New Year's Eve. Anyone have suggestions on any affordable places to stay?" We sat back and waited.

Five minutes went by, and her computer dinged with a Facebook message. One of her college friends who lived in New York City explained to my wife how she and her husband hated being in New York City over New Year's Eve, so they were heading to Florida for the weekend. They had an apartment on the other side of the river. We could stay there if we agreed to feed their birds and rabbit. My wife's eyes grew as big as quarters, and she started to shake as she responded that we would be happy to feed her pets in exchange for a place to stay. Iowa State went on to lose the game, but we had an unforgettable night in Times Square and an even better trip because my wife asked for help.

I received a gentle reminder of this philosophy in the spring of 2017. My close friend, Anthony Paustian, was in the process of putting together his final speaker lineup for an annual event he hosts called ciLive! (Celebrate Innovation Live). Tony is the founder of ciLive!, and he hosts this event to bring in speakers from all over the country to inspire the next generation and celebrate innovation. Previous speakers include Apollo astronauts, hosts of TV shows, Sci-Fi movie stars, special effects artists, and more. This particular year, he was bringing in an Apollo astronaut named Al Worden.

Al had been the command module pilot for Apollo 15. His job was to fly to the moon with two other astronauts, launch their craft to the surface of the moon, and then orbit the moon for three days while they did their work. At the end of the three days, they boarded their craft and launched back into space. It was Al's time to shine as he had to meet up with the lunar crew in orbit around the Moon and dock his command module with their craft. The three men then made their way back to Earth.

I came home after Tony had told me this story and relayed it almost verbatim to my wife. She got a huge smile on her face and asked, "Do you think he would be willing to come and speak to my kindergarten class?" I paused and laughed in her face.

Before you judge me too hard, at the time, Kacey taught kindergarten at Dallas Center Elementary, a school in a town of around 2,000 people. Her class had about 22 students, and there was only one other kindergarten class of about 20 more kids. In my mind, it would be a waste of time to see if the famous Apollo astronaut would take time out of his day to speak to such a small group of kids. Kacey did not see it that way.

"Mr. Beyer," she said as she looked over the top of her glasses. I always know I am in trouble when she calls me "Mr. Beyer." "You tell people all the time to ask people what they want. You're not even going to try?" She had me there. I picked up my phone and called Tony to see if Al would be willing to speak to Kacey's class. He laughed as hard as I had. After he calmed down, he said he would ask but not to hold my breath. About 15 minutes later, I got a text — "If your wife can have her classroom ready at 9:00 a.m. on Tuesday, he'll be there."

I was in shock, and so was Kacey. We confirmed the visit with the principal, and Tuesday morning I showed up with Tony to drive Al to Dallas Center Elementary. We pulled up to the building a little before 9:00 a.m., and a banner across the front of the entry read, "Welcome Astronaut Worden." My wife met us at the entrance and shook Al's hand, a smug smile on her face as she made eye contact with me. We made our way to the library, and both classes of kids were sitting on the floor with astronaut helmets made out of milk jugs.

For the next hour, Al told the kids stories of what it was like to fly to space and be alone in the command module while the other astronauts were on the moon. He confirmed that the Moon was, in fact, not made out of cheese and answered all kinds of questions from the kids ranging from "How did you become an astronaut?" to "How did you poop up there?" He ended his time by explaining that he fully believed that the kids in that room would be in the generation who would eventually land on Mars. All this took place because of a simple ask of a stranger.

The best thing I learned over the years is that most people want to help others succeed. They want a part in creating something great, and they enjoy seeing others achieve happiness without expecting anything in return. The problem is that we cannot help people when we do not know what they want. To solve this problem, we must make our desires known. We cannot expect others to read our minds.

As my examples show, even strangers and long-lost friends are willing to help if they believe in the message and see value in what you want to accomplish. Mitch and I barely knew each other when we met for coffee, but he gave me everything I needed to launch a new speaking career. My wife had not talked with her college girlfriend in years, but her friend was more than willing to open her apartment to us. Al was another stranger but was willing to give of his time simply to inspire a new generation of astronauts. Sharing dreams and ideas is not always easy, but as Erma Bombeck, the famous author and columnist, put it, "It takes a lot of courage to show your dreams to someone else." Find that courage and share your dream. You never know how the person sitting across from you might be able to help.

Tell People What You Want

Most of us have dreams, goals, or desires. Unfortunately, we tend to keep these things to ourselves. The biggest benefit of having a network is the ability for others to help you achieve those things you want most out of life. Write down two to three goals you think your network can help you achieve, and be sure to include why you want to accomplish them. Then tell anyone who will listen about these goals. You'll be surprised how many people will be willing to help!

1. Goal 1:

_____

_____

_____

_____

_____

_____

_____

2. Goal 2:

_____

_____

_____

_____

_____

_____

_____

3. Goal 3:

_____

_____

_____

_____

_____

_____

_____

4. Goal 4:

_____

_____

_____

_____

_____

_____

Get Over Being Nice

I shared the message about making sure people know what you want to a group of non-profit directors. They asked me to talk about networking and how to get the most out of their existing networks. As the presentation came to a close, I asked for questions. One of the attendees, the director of a non-profit, shot her hand in the air and asked the following: "I have a close friend who knows a person I would like to meet. I think this person could have a great impact on my organization and the people we serve. But I do not want my friend to think I am using her. What is the best way to ask for the introduction without making my friend think I am using her?"

At the time, this question took me by surprise, but as I reflected on it, I realized others were thinking the same thing. None of us want our friends to think we are only friends because of their connections or the things we need from them. We do not want to come off sales-y, arrogant, or self-serving. In short, we want to be nice.

After careful consideration, I turned to the director and told her I was confused by her question. First, she told me she had a close friend. Second, she said she needed an introduction to a person who could greatly impact her organization. Something was not adding up. Either her friend was not as close as she let on, or the person she wanted to be introduced to was not that important. She looked mildly confused and upset.

Sensing her discomfort, I ran a different scenario by her. What would she do if her friend asked her for a similar introduction? Would she be willing to introduce her friend to a connection? She smiled, "Of course, I would." She stated she would do anything to help her friend. I replied, "Can I tell you a secret? That is exactly how your friend feels." I saw the light bulb come on. Later, I received an upbeat email from the director informing me she had called her friend and asked for the introduction. Her friend was more than happy to help, and the director secured an appointment for the following week.

I have told this story to hundreds of organizations and groups. After one such talk, a gentleman approached me and shared his view on asking for favors or sharing dreams with friends: "I liked your story about the lady who was afraid to ask her friend for an introduction. I used to have the same mindset until one of my mentors gave me a fresh perspective. Instead of worrying about friends thinking I am using them, I now realize I am holding back an opportunity from someone who wants to help me. If I had a friend whom I could help achieve something great but did not know about it because my friend never told me how I could assist, I would be offended. It would tell me they did not think I was a trusted or valued friend. Why would we want to hold back opportunities from our friends who want to help us more than anyone else?"

Do you suffer from being too nice? Are you, like the director, worried about people thinking you are using them? My best piece of advice: get over it. People genuinely want to help, and the only way they can is if we let them know what we want. We have to share our goals and dreams to let others know how they can help make those dreams a reality. Make that phone call, ask for that introduction, or share that dream because it is the only way others can help.

How Can I Help You?

At the end of every meeting, whether it is with a new connection or an old friend, I ask a variation of "How can I help you?" This question catches people off guard. A typical response usually involves an awkward smile or laugh accompanied with a brush-off phrase like, "Oh, I'm good. Thank you, though," or "Don't worry about it. I'm okay." Occasionally, someone asks for clarification, as if I asked the question in a foreign language. I smile and explain that I am genuinely interested in helping if anything comes up. A few moments of silence pass as they digest. Inevitably, something comes to mind, and they ask.

It is amazing the stories and experiences people share when they are asked if they need help. I have been asked for things ranging from introductions to helping with fundraisers to finding volunteers to being a mentor. One of my favorites came after a talk I gave on networking to a workforce development organization. The crowd was small, so we had an intimate and honest discussion. I explained my philosophy on helping others, and afterward, I was approached by a young lady who had recently moved to town. She explained what she was trying to accomplish after taking a new job. She then thanked me for my time and asked if it would be OK if she emailed me with questions. Of course, it was.

The following week, I received an email explaining several ways I could help her. She needed to know where she could meet new people and make new friends. She wanted to write a book and wanted to talk about the process and meet my publisher. She wanted to try skydiving, and she was interested in getting some feedback on doing modeling on the side. At the end, she apologized for the "novel" she had written, but she wanted to take full advantage of the opportunity if I could help her in any way. That afternoon, I got to work.

I set up a meeting between her and my publisher, and we had coffee to talk about writing a book. I provided several resources for networking opportunities and ways to get engaged with the community. We talked about how a close friend of mine had gone skydiving and was close to solo jumping at a municipal airport. I even introduced her to a modeling agency.

My favorite "how can I help you moment" happened in the summer of 2015. One of my friends had sent an introduction email connecting me with a woman named Melanie Menken, the president of a non-profit named Booster Pak. I scheduled the coffee, and we had a delightful conversation about who she was and why she had started Booster Pak in the first place.

She explained that her organization worked in conjunction with the "free and reduced meals" program at the West Des Moines school district. The program provides breakfast and lunch to children in need throughout the district. It is a great program that provides a valuable service, but it could only provide food during school hours. It turned out kids were not getting regular meals on nights and weekends, and that was leading to behavior issues. As she put it, kids were coming to school hungry on Monday, and they would act out. Toward the middle of the week, the hunger would subside, and they would be able to focus on school again. Her program was there to fill the void and get those same kids food on nights and weekends.

Her story touched my heart, being married to a kindergarten teacher and all. The meeting was ending, and I asked how I could help her. She got a giant smile on her face and said, "I knew you would ask that. The person who connected us told me you would ask that, and I have something for you!"

She went on to explain that her program was having wild

success with younger kids, but they saw a significant drop off as children got older, and by fourth grade, most kids were no longer coming to get food. It turns out that's when kids really start to notice when someone is "different" from the norm, so the kids had the choice to either "be normal" and go hungry or pick up food at the end of the day from Booster Pak and get made fun of. Most kids just want to be normal, so they went hungry.

My heart broke, and I stressed again that I wanted to help. Melanie had a simple request. She wanted around fifty drawstring backpacks that she could put the food in. Something nondescript so it could look like the kids were carrying around anything, books, shoes, gym clothes. That would help clear the burden of carrying a plastic grocery sack of food and hopefully keep kids coming to the program.

I admitted that I did not have fifty, but I had five she could have right away. She smiled and said she understood but appreciated anything I could do to help her reach her goal. As I drove back to my office, I decided to share her story and ask on Facebook. The post was simple and to the point—I told people I needed drawstring backpacks for a local non-profit and a good cause. Messages started to come in with people offering bags they had sitting in their closet, much like myself. I knew it might take a while to get to fifty, but we would eventually get there.

Later that same afternoon, my phone rang with a number I didn't recognize. I answered and learned that the caller was a friend of my brother's and wanted to know what I was doing with the backpacks. I explained the situation, and he told me he wanted to help. The previous weekend he had hosted a 5k and had about 200 drawstring backpacks that he didn't need. They were insulated and labeled with a name-brand shoe logo. He asked if I thought those would work. I excitedly exclaimed that they were perfect and asked where I could meet him to pick them up.

"Don't worry about it. I'm out running some errands right now anyway. What's her address and I'll just drop them off on her doorstep."

I didn't even have to meet him; he was willing to help a stranger because he felt it was the right thing to do. Kids were able to get food and eat simply because of one meeting and one Facebook post. That's the power of the question "How can I help you?" combined with telling people what you want.

Offering to help need not be a huge commitment or burden, and it is not meant to be. I shared these stories because I was able to help the young woman with her dreams with only an hour of my time and a couple of follow-up emails. It took another coffee and about seven minutes of Facebook and phone time to get meals to kids who needed them. You'll be surprised at the opportunities that present themselves when you're willing to help.

"Do What You Say You Will Do."

One of the best ways to build trust is to lend a helping hand whenever possible. One of the fastest ways to damage that trust is to fail to follow through. Not only does it leave the other party let down, but it also sets the initial impression of unreliability. Once this impression is set, it is sometimes impossible to overcome.

Plenty of individuals are talkers. They say they are willing to help. They make promises and appointments, but they never follow through. I have no doubt their initial intentions were good, but life gets in the way. Soon, soccer practice, work, volunteer activities, or thousands of other priorities come up, and it gets harder to follow through on past commitments that do not seem as important as others. Priorities shift, people forget, and suddenly, that offer to help passes without a second thought.

Author and speaker Adam Carroll gave a presentation that stuck with me for years. The talk centered on building real relationships both in business and personal life. He used the phrase that is the header of this section: "Do what you say you will do." During the talk, he explained that following through on promises, whether it meant picking up a gallon of milk from the store or introducing someone to the President of the United States, is what separates those who build great reputations from those who do not. By doing what you say you will, or as Adam says, "DWYSYWD," you separate yourself from the average person and begin the journey to being great.

To stick to the philosophy of doing what you say you will, do not overcommit. Do not make promises or commitments that are outside your ability, your time, your financial means, or your desires. It is easier to set expectations from the beginning than to explain why they were not met in the end.

Once, I had coffee with the director of a local non-profit.

She wanted to meet and talk about fundraising strategies and volunteer opportunities. We went through the mission of the organization and how they were making a difference in the community. Then came her question. She wanted to know if I would be interested in helping her raise $5,000 over 30 days as a kickoff to a large campaign.

My heart jumped at the opportunity, but my head told me to slow down and evaluate. Did I have the time to commit to this project? Did I have the passion? Could I follow through if I committed to raising $5,000? In the end, I knew the answer to these questions was no, but I did want to help her and her program succeed.

I offered a compromise. I explained that I wanted to help her, and I felt a real connection with what she was doing. I also explained how other engagements and previous commitments would keep me from devoting the required attention to achieving her goal. I asked if it was OK if I committed to helping her raise $1,000 of her $5,000 goal.

I saw she was slightly disappointed but knew she did not want to pass up the opportunity. We set up a plan complete with a deadline for raising the $1,000 I committed to. I gave her the names of four individuals who might be willing to help raise $1,000 apiece. She spoke with them, and in the end, our combined efforts helped her hit her $5,000 goal two weeks earlier than anticipated. She was grateful for the introductions and for the help. I felt good because I made a reasonable commitment and followed through.

Sometimes doing what you say you will do can also stretch you and help you achieve things you didn't know were possible. I ran for Dallas Center City Council in the fall of 2015 and was elected to my first term. The city and community had been working for years to build a new library or remodel the existing one to add additional programming and children's spaces. Studies had been done, funds had been raised, and plans drawn up. The project moved forward, slower than most wanted, but it kept going.

During a library board meeting in the summer of 2019, one of the board members questioned if we really could raise the remaining million or so dollars through donations. He wasn't sure the community itself could put up the money. Something about his comments rubbed me the wrong way, and I stated that I believed in the community of Dallas Center and that we would be breaking ground by the summer of 2020 on a new library. The board and individuals in attendance looked at me with shock on their faces. I had effectively just volunteered to be the chief fundraiser to bring this project to a conclusion.

We put together a final fundraising committee and got to work gathering names of individuals we thought could write checks and businesses we wanted to prospect. Additional funds started to come in, and we quickly had about half of the funds raised. I put together a grant proposal for one of the larger Prairie Meadows Legacy Grants and was confident that our presentation would push us over the edge. The final interviews were set for in-person meetings in March of 2020. We all know what happened next…

Due to the pandemic, the grant process got delayed to 2021. I wasn't sure what we were going to do, given that in-person meetings were on an indefinite hold, and people seemed to be holding onto their money tighter than ever before. No one knew what would happen next. With a heavy heart, I realized that we would not be breaking ground during the summer of 2020, but with any luck, we could hopefully start the summer of 2021.

The library director asked the Council if she could start part of the interior remodel since we had the funds available. We approved the design, and the project went out for construction bids. What we thought was going to be a $125,000 project came in at just over $60,000. The labor market was repressed, and people were hungry for work. We approved the bid, and I got on the phone with the library director and design architect to ask them how quickly we could get the rest of the library design done and out to bid. This was a once-in-a-lifetime opportunity, and we weren't going to miss it.

We moved forward and put the entire project out to bid just before the inflation jump on lumber and steel. The bids came back close to 30% less than we expected. We had enough cash in the bank, and shovels went into the ground in late summer 2020. I had held true to my word.

No one had any idea in the summer of 2019 when I made the claim that we would be building by 2020 that everything would happen in the way that it did. Sometimes, all it takes is putting an idea or thought out in the universe to see what happens. People jumped on the cause to see the library project come to a close and the community is better for it.

Building solid relationships takes time and building trust

takes repeated positive experiences. Following through with the commitments you make helps this. Do not overcommit. Give people options if they ask too much or if you know you cannot commit. It is better to follow through on a smaller commitment than to fail at a larger one, and occasionally it's fun to throw something big out there just to see what you can accomplish.

CHAPTER 7

INCREASING YOUR INFLUENCE

Want More? Do More!

Organizations are always looking for enthusiastic and willing volunteers. Most of these organizations also provide opportunities for beneficial networking events. They create chances for people to connect through socials, fundraisers, charity events, small group meetings, board positions, and more. Some of the best networking takes place during these meetings when there is no formal networking component on the agenda. This is the reason I encourage everyone to find an organization they are passionate about and get involved.

I began attending chamber of commerce functions in 2009 as a way to meet people and build my sales business. I found my circle of friends expanding to include more chamber people. Evenings and weekends filled up with social activities involving this new group of networking friends. I learned more about the chamber and its purpose in our community through these relationships. The goal of the chamber—to foster business relationships and help members connect and succeed—fit nicely with my personal beliefs and goals. I decided to get more involved.

Earlier, I gave away the secret to getting involved. However, I get asked so many times how I got involved that it is necessary to repeat it.

The easiest way to get involved is to tell people what you want. Find the leaders of the organization and explain how you want to take an active role. Ask those leaders what opportunities exist. If you have a direct position you want to apply for or a specific event you want to help with, make that clear.

My first conversation with the chamber president resulted in me applying to become an ambassador. This role required more of my time because it came with the expectation that I would attend at least 60 percent of chamber functions. This requirement opened many doors because it forced me to meet additional members while actively engaging new members. I served as an ambassador for two years, attending events and expanding my network. After proving myself and meeting expectations, I asked for a position on the board.

That appointment happened the following year, and doors

continued to open. I met more of the membership and continued to expand my professional and personal networks. The board position came with more responsibilities, which I embraced. In 2014, I was appointed to the executive board and served as the Chamber chair in 2017. The opportunities this appointment provided were incredible, and it all started because I asked how I could become more involved.

Getting involved in any organization you are passionate about will open doors and afford you opportunities you never knew existed. The phrase "you get out of it what you put in" may be overused, but it is 100 percent true in this case. The fastest way to make an impact and benefit from being a member of any organization is to show up. As one of my closest personal friends, Christopher Maharry, is apt to say, "90% of life is showing up." Volunteer and let people know you want to help and be involved. You will immediately become more recognizable, and people will begin to rely on you. Be sure to do what you say you will do and follow through on all commitments. This will ensure success within the organization and provide additional opportunities down the road.

Don't Forget About Me...

Have you ever walked into an event and immediately recognized a person but cannot figure out why or how you know them? You make eye contact, and see the same struggle on their face. They know you too, but neither of you know why. Maybe you exchange an awkward wave or a head nod to acknowledge you have seen each other. Maybe one of you is brave enough to re-introduce yourself. More than likely, you both avoid contact and spend the rest of the event ignoring one another, so neither of you appears as if you have forgotten who the other is. The event ends, and you both leave, never knowing how or why you know each other.

This exact thing happened to me at one of the first events I attended. I walked into a small networking group and was immediately drawn to a woman across the table. We made eye contact, and I could tell she was thinking the same thing. We knew each other, but from where? Luckily, this group required introductions, so I heard her name, and she heard mine. The meeting closed, and we walked up to each other to figure out the mystery. It took us almost a year to realize we had been in the same Dale Carnegie class seven years prior.

The case of the lost or forgotten connection is common. I read a great article about the three types of "ties" we have in our networks. Adam Grant, a business professor at the Wharton School of Business, explains that most of us recognize or have heard about "weak" ties and "strong" ties, but we often forget about the third type called "dormant" ties.[14] He explains that these ties may have been strong at one point but became dormant due to lack of follow-up or changes in priorities. We spend our lives meeting new people, and it is easy to forget someone we have not seen in a while. As our networks grow, it becomes harder to make sure we stay in contact with everyone we meet, but it can be done.

The easiest way to stay on top of the different connections we have is to segment them into buckets. The point of segmenting these relationships is to give us the opportunity to create a follow-up or contact plan. The buckets that make the biggest impact on our lives or require the most attention, both professionally and personally, receive higher priority. The buckets I use are the following:

Referral resources: These connections are ones with whom I actively pass business back and forth. We build strong relationships and a high level of trust. These relationships are vital to my sales business and make my life easier. They also afford me the greatest opportunities to help others. I make it a priority to keep in touch with these people at least once a month, whether it is through a phone call, email, text, tweet, or face-to-face meeting.

Business: Business connections are not as strong as referral resources. They are individuals I may or may not do business with, but they provide other professional opportunities. They include individuals I turn to for advice, share success stories with, and with whom I am comfortable working if the chance arises. I contact these people once a quarter to check in and find out if there is a chance for us to strengthen our relationships. As time goes on, I have moved people from the business bucket to the referral bucket and vice versa.

Personal: Personal relationships are friends and family members. I know business will more than likely never be done with these individuals, but I like hanging out with them. They are people I have the most in common with and people whose company I enjoy. We may have a long history, and reconnecting after a period of time without seeing one another can happen immediately. I talk to most of these people on a weekly basis, if not daily. There are a few exceptions when friends move or situations change, but overall, these are the people who surround me outside of work.

Just-for-fun: The just-for-fun bucket is just that. This bucket holds the bulk of newer relationships and people who do not clearly fit into one of the other buckets. It includes acquaintances, new business connections, and those who have fallen out of one of the other buckets. This bucket is the hardest to manage because it also has the most potential for growth. I weigh each relationship inside the just-for-fun bucket differently because of this potential. Follow-ups and contacts depend on what bucket I see the new connection most easily falling into in the future.

As you can imagine, there is some crossover between buckets. Some of my best referral partners are also some of my closest friends. This tends to happen as relationships form and trust builds. As we build relationships and foster trust, we are sincerely drawn to one another. It becomes easier to refer business when we find out who that person is outside of work. When we learn about each other's families, hobbies, passions, and create real connections, business always follows.

The great thing about the bucket system is its fluidity. Individuals move in and out of buckets depending on how the relationship functions at any given moment. The end goal is always to move people into higher buckets until they reach the one that makes the most sense for that relationship. Most new connections start in the just-for-fun bucket with the goal of moving them into one of the three higher buckets. It is only through developing those new relationships that we learn where they belong.

The four buckets I use will not work for everyone. I encourage you to take a look at your connections and figure out a similar system. I also recommend having no more than five different buckets at any one time. The more segmented the relationships, the harder and more complex the follow-up system becomes. By keeping it simple, there is a greater chance for success and a higher probability that a connection will not go dormant.

As the world continues to become more connected and there are more ways than ever to keep in touch with others, another strategy has surfaced that I find myself using almost daily. I call it the "Divine Intervention" strategy.

Unlike the bucket system, this follow-up or check-in system relies solely on intuition or following your gut on reach-outs. A simple example—have you ever been driving your car or reading a book, and a random person popped into your head? You could have been doing something completely unrelated, and a name or a face will just appear without warning. This is a moment of divine intervention. Something in your subconscious is telling you to reach out or check in on that person.

When this happens, I will send a simple email, text message, LinkedIn message, or other form of communication and let the person know I was just thinking about them. Depending on the context, the messaging will center on checking in or asking for a meeting to catch up and reconnect. This isn't the most sophisticated approach, but it does make people feel important, knowing that others are thinking about them in a completely genuine way. Listen to that voice in your head; it's often trying to tell you something for a good reason.

My favorite example of this follow-up approach took place shortly after I changed careers and started working at Iron Horse. A friend I hadn't spoken to in a while randomly popped into my head while I was on a conference call. I couldn't reach out immediately, so I sent myself an email as a reminder to text the person later that day. The call ended, and I texted my friend with a simple check-in message.

"Hey, I was just thinking about you and wondered how life was going. Any chance we can get together sometime soon and catch up?"

A couple of minutes later came the reply, "Hey man, yeah, that'd be good. I know a lot has changed for both of us, and it would be good to get together."

We set the coffee meeting and got together in person a couple of days later. The conversation was pretty typical, with updates about family, careers, trips, and general life events. Towards the end, he explained he was glad I reached out because he had some questions about some investments he had. He wasn't sure where to turn as he didn't think he had enough assets for an advisor to work with him. I told him to send me some statements and additional information so we could see what needed to be done. Shortly after that meeting, he became a client and has since sent me additional referrals. Something in my subconscious brought this person to mind, and I'm glad I listened. We're still working together, and our bond has never been stronger, simply because of some divine intervention. The next time someone randomly appears in your thoughts, try reaching out. You might be surprised by the opportunities that present themselves.

Connecting and Reconnecting

A network is only as good as your best connections. Weak connections tend to forget you as quickly as you forget about them. Are there people from high school, college, old jobs, or past organizations you haven't talked with in a while? Go ahead and reach out to them and rekindle some old connections. Turn those weak relationships into strong ones again.

List one to two people from each of the following areas that you would like to reconnect with and do it!

1. High school

_____

_____

2. College

_____

_____

3. Past employment

_____

_____

4. Volunteer or civic organizations

_____

_____

5. Divine Intervention/Other

_____

_____

_____

_____

The Written Word

A stranger sent me an email in late 2012 asking to take me to coffee. He wanted to get to know me as well as share information about the business he was in. He also explained how he was newer to town and trying to figure out how to connect with people. Sticking to the "first meeting is free" philosophy, I happily agreed to meet him. We had a great discussion about his goals and dreams, what he did for a living, and how I could help him get more involved in the community. He asked me all the right questions, and I left feeling like I had made a great new connection. He was immediately put in my business bucket, and I made a note to follow up with him a couple of months later to see his progress.

Two days later, I strolled into my office and saw a little

white envelope sitting in my mail slot. I do not know about you, but I love getting mail. It is like Christmas morning. I cannot wait to rip it open and see what exciting surprise rests inside. To say I was excited was an understatement. I rushed over and saw that the envelope was from the gentleman I had coffee with two days prior. My curiosity piqued as I opened it and found a handwritten thank-you card inside.

The card was nothing spectacular, just a simple printed "thank you" across the front. Inside the card, he hand-wrote a few sentences thanking me for my time and explaining how he was planning to implement some of the things we discussed. He concluded by thanking me one more time and emphasizing that he was excited for the next opportunity for us to connect. It was wonderful.

My new connection could just as easily have sent an email, message, or text, which would have taken 30 seconds to compose and send. Instead, he took time from his busy schedule to craft a handwritten letter of thanks. That letter had an immediate impact on me and my day. It showed a genuineness that is often missing from most social interactions. It made him stand out among a sea of emails. Here was someone different, someone who cared about building relationships.

I have tried sending a thank-you card after every meeting since receiving that note in 2012. The meeting need not be business-related to justify the time for a thank-you note. A cup of coffee with a new connection, reconnecting with an old friend, and checking in with a business relationship all warrant thank-you notes. They are simple pieces of paper, but they make an immediate impact. They show that you care and are not too busy to let someone know how much you appreciate them.

The best part of writing thank-you notes is that they do not take much time, and the impact far outweighs that time commitment. A good thank-you note has six steps:

- Greeting such as a hello or the person's name
- Expression of thanks
- Specific details about the meeting or connection
- An explanation of how you plan on taking action from the meeting
- Restate thanks
- Closing such as stating you look forward to seeing them soon or other statement

I do not know if the person I met with in 2012 knew these steps or had been taught them during his career. I do know his simple note was clear, concise, and made a lasting impact on how I follow up with connections. His act opened my eyes to the power of the written word. I have sent hundreds of thank-you notes after opening his card. Many times, I never hear if the person received the card or not. Occasionally, I will get one back. There have even been times when I get a phone call just for the person to express their thanks for the time I took to write them.

The next time you have a meeting, try sending a thank-you card. There is a good chance you will never hear from the other person, but know you have made a difference and possibly made someone's day better.

Wrap Up

We all have connections and networks. The size of those networks does not matter; it does matter how we harness those relationships. By becoming conscious that networking happens around us all of the time and by realizing these connections exist, we can put them to work for others and ourselves. Always be willing to help others and connect individuals. Take meetings when they are requested; "the first meeting is free; you have to earn the second" should be a constant reminder that we have something to learn from each other. Give people the attention they deserve and put distracting cell phones or other devices to the side. Get involved and send handwritten thank-you notes. Most importantly, tell people what you want. These suggestions ensure you will get more out of your network.

CHAPTER 8

An Introduction to Networking in the Digital Age

The final section of this book covers using social media and networking in a digital age. As stated earlier, the biggest overhaul of this edition will be found in the following pages. I still believe that face-to-face interaction is crucial to building long-term, beneficial relationships, but I've also learned that much more can be accomplished through a Zoom meeting than I ever thought possible. The pandemic pushed our use and acceptance of digital networking decades into the future in a truly short amount of time. Social media can still be a great tool to connect and facilitate in-person meetings, but it can also be used to build trusting and lasting relationships with people on the other side of the screen.

The Only Constant is Change

I open this section with the header "the only constant is change" because it holds true in life but more so in the landscape of social media and digital relationships. Most of the technology and platforms we enjoy today did not exist at the beginning of the new century. New platforms are added each year. The most popular sites are infants compared to established businesses. LinkedIn was founded in 2003, and Facebook in 2004. Twitter came out in 2006, and Instagram and Pinterest hit the market in 2010 and 2011, respectively.[16] Snapchat entered the scene in late 2011, and TikTok came along five years later in 2016. Although they are all new businesses, their impact on marketing, connecting, and building relationships has been dramatic.

According to data released by Statusbrew.com in December of 2021, Facebook was quickly approaching 3 billion users with 2.8 billion daily active users.[17] They also share a parent company with WhatsApp, Instagram, and Messenger, which rank 3, 4, and 5 in total users. LinkedIn has crossed over 800 million users worldwide and holds the perception as the leading social media platform in the professional world. Twitter has just under 400 million users and is largely considered, along with Tik Tok, where social media trends start. For additional context, social media ad spend increased around 12.7% in 2021, and 63% of customers now expect businesses to offer customer service support through social media. Instagram continues to lead the way for business engagement, and the average individual will spend over two hours a day on various platforms.

These staggering numbers, and the fact that social media allows anyone with an internet connection to unite with individuals and businesses worldwide, are validation enough for a specific section in a networking book. The doors these tools open, coupled with their impact on almost every person's daily life, make them essential. The problem with adding this section is that it will be out of date before it is published because the platforms change, and users will migrate as better apps are created. Each new app is an improvement on an existing feature and has its own appeal for attracting new members. Luckily for us, while the platforms change, the value they deliver will be the same. In the end, they allow individuals to connect openly and share content freely with one another on a massive scale.

Prior to 2020, most of us had heard of Zoom but didn't use it regularly, let alone know where the mute button was. The phrase "you're on mute" or "we can't hear you" became commonplace in my household during virtual business meetings and at-home learning. We still joke when someone accidentally starts talking before taking themselves off mute, but we all have become relatively efficient in the tools and connectivity the platform provides. And, like it or not, life and business continued in large part due to the connectivity Zoom and platforms like it offered. It is now common in our working world and in our lives and will continue to be an integral part of relationships moving forward. Because of this, I have added a section covering connecting and networking through digital means when face-to-face meetings aren't an option or a preferred method of communication. As part of social media, I will cover Facebook, LinkedIn, and Twitter due to their current rankings, potential for business interaction, and ability to create online brands. Each offers unique opportunities for individuals and businesses depending on their goals and objectives. They continue to be some of the most used apps in the market and the ones with which I have seen personal and professional success. All offer different user experiences and can be used in various situations depending on the desired outcome.

However, before I discuss Facebook, I need to mention two topics that are more important. These things separate the average user from those who get immediate and direct results. They also continue to be the two things that have remained constant since the release of the first edition of this book. While platforms have changed - we've seen videos rise to prominence, and algorithms that seem to shift daily, if not hourly - two core things have remained the same. It turns out it is not about the profile picture you use or a great hashtag, the two things that matter most are content and consistency.

If You Can't Say Something Valuable...

Bambi is one of Disney's all-time classics. The traumatic experience of Bambi losing his mom to hunters is most children's first experience with death and opens up the door for parents to talk with their kids about this difficult subject. One of the less talked about scenes in *Bambi* teaches another valuable lesson. When Thumper first meets Bambi, he asks Bambi's mother what she will name him. After she says, "Bambi," Thumper looks at her and says, "That's a funny name." This earns Thumper a scolding with his mom asking what his father told him that morning. Thumper responds, "If you can't say something nice, don't say nothin' at all!"

This lesson holds true for social media content, albeit with a minor change. If you cannot say something *valuable*, don't say anything at all. It may sound harsh, and, yes, the majority of social media interaction is people sharing useless information, but the purpose of this chapter is to make social media work for you. In order to expand your influence and become recognizable on social media, you have to post or share valuable, usable content. It will separate you from the majority who post less than useful information or continually get in political fights online.

Sharing useful content is easier than most people think. Some of the most successful individuals on social media are not sharing earth-shattering ideas or directing missions to Mars. They are posting the things they are truly passionate about and sharing that passion with others who have similar interests. When people are passionate, that passion shows, and that is what makes those posts fun to read.

In the second section of this book, I wrote about finding people's stories and asking about their passions. We also talked about how this allows you to share your story and tell others about your passions. The story you came up with in that section is a good starting point for finding what you should post. Finding this passion or story makes the rest of the process easier. It also provides guidance when you have trouble figuring out what to say. Find that passion, and the content almost creates itself. Writer's block will happen even with a great story or compelling passion. Luckily, other people have ideas for creating content when this happens. One of my favorite infographics shows 22 ways to create great, compelling content.[18] With this infographic, Brian Clark shows how simple exercises like asking your readers for ideas, inviting a guest writer to post, or writing a review can jumpstart the creative process.

Creating great content does not mean it must be truly significant or mind-altering. It simply needs to be well-thought-out and valuable to your audience. In fact, it doesn't need to be your content at all. It also helps to read or watch what others in the industry are posting. My best content comes from leaders in the industry. I love to repin, retweet, and share great articles or ideas from these leaders. It also helps me learn what the market is currently interested in instead of going on my own random musings. With social media, it is incredibly easy to find these leaders. Chances are you are already following them or have liked their Facebook pages. If not, find out who these leaders are and use their content to springboard your creativity.

The most important thing to realize with content is that not everything will go viral. Worrying about what to create takes more time than creating it. Too many people spend too much time thinking about what they are going to create instead of creating it. There is no guaranteed success rate with each post, video, blog, tweet, or pin. The easiest way to get over this and start creating great content is to find your passion and start writing, taking pictures, recording videos, or experimenting with media. Each best-selling book starts with the first letter, each chart-topping song with the first note, and each blockbuster movie with the first scene. What will be your first step?

Be Consistent, or Pay the Price

We all have the opportunity to be unique brands through social media. Think about that for a second. Every single person with an internet connection has the opportunity to brand themselves as Nike branded the Swoosh, Coca-Cola branded the red and white soda can, or Apple branded the apple. All it takes is great content, time, and consistency.

The rise of the "influencer" or "micro-influencer" only strengthens this point. As a teacher, my wife often asks her kindergarten students what they want to be when they grow up. In recent years she has seen a shift from "fireman," "astronaut," or "teacher" to professions like "YouTube star," "social media influencer," or "TikTok famous." Kids as young as five years old see the impact that social media is having not only on their daily lives but on their parents' lives as well. Influencers are being paid to simply try products on their channels so that the brand gets some recognition. It's never been easier to get paid for having a personal brand.

Providing a consistent message is second only to the

message or content itself. Consistency in branding and the messages make the above images so iconic. Each of those corporations owns the brand recognition associated with them without question because they never varied from their messages or the associated images. Their consistency created a mental connection with the images and brands unto themselves. This is the power of branding, and creating a personal brand is just as important.

I worked hard over the years to create a brand for myself in my community. I am a well-respected businessperson who works tirelessly to connect people and make my community a better place. However, one night in 2013, I had a lapse in judgment. It was the kickoff to Sunday Night Football and the unveiling of Carrie Underwood as Faith Hill's replacement for singing the opening credits. I was excited to post my impressions of the new opening on Facebook and Twitter. What happened next serves as a reminder to watch what I post.

Underwood took the stage, and I remember being blown away by how chiseled her legs were. I like to run and work out, and I would kill to have legs like that. I was in awe of how much time and discipline it must have taken her to get those results. Now, if I had posted something along those lines, I am sure everything would have been fine. Instead, I posted, "I want to touch Carrie Underwood's legs." The backlash was swift and immediate. Close friends texted to make sure things were OK between my wife and me. Emails came in telling me I needed to watch what I posted online. Weeks went by with people scolding me at chamber functions, in restaurants, and at work, all because of a seven-word Facebook post I thought was innocent at the time.

This example not only shows the power of being inconsistent, but it also shows the reach social media has. That post went so against what I typically post that it caught people's attention immediately. In essence, that post went viral because of its lack of consistency with what I had been posting up to that point. Friends of friends of friends saw that post and were compelled to ask me about it. I still wonder how many people saw those seven words because, for each individual who called me out, there were countless others who did not.

All it takes is one inconsistent post or comment to tear down everything built before it. Alina Tugend points out in her *NY Times* article, "Praise is Fleeting, but Brickbats We Recall," that research shows time and time again how individuals are more likely to remember negative experiences than positive ones. One experiment points out that people are more upset about losing 50 dollars than they are happy about winning 50 dollars.[19] Do not give your audience the opportunity to have that negative experience by being inconsistent with the message or brand you are trying to create.

In the end, content and consistency will make the biggest impact on how social media strengthens your network and builds your personal brand. It will not matter how many times a day you post to each platform or how many followers you have if the content is not valuable and consistent. Figure out these two things, and the doors will open wide.

Social Media Tips

It is easy to become overwhelmed with the number of social media platforms that are available. To that end, we will focus on three specific platforms – Facebook, Twitter, and LinkedIn. Below are some things to think about regarding each platform and its benefits.

General items that can be applied to any platform:

1. Who is my target audience?

_____

_____

_____

_____

2. Will I be creating my own content or predominately sharing others' content?

_____

_____

_____

_____

3. Will I be using the platform for personal reasons, professional reasons, or both?

_____

_____

_____

_____

4. What is my end goal with being on the platform?

_____

_____

_____

_____

CHAPTER 9

Networking with Facebook

We have already covered some of the staggering statistics that go with the largest social media platform currently in existence: Facebook. It is mind-blowing how one company can have a massive global impact in a relatively short amount of time. In 10 years, Facebook managed to infiltrate over a billion people's lives and continues to grow each year. In fact, the number of users has doubled in the last five years. Facebook demographics indicate it is becoming an "older" platform, with more individuals between the ages of 25-34 using the platform followed by those aged 18-23. The teen market is more active on other platforms, but there is still plenty of user engagement. In fact, removing Google's preloaded apps on Android devices as a variable, the four most downloaded apps on the Google Play Store are all affiliated with Facebook. In short, Facebook is where you need to be to get the most out of social networking and to expand your brand.[20]

The problem with Facebook is that they are always changing the rules. In the beginning, many functions and features were free. It was simple for a small business or individual to build a page, do a little advertising, create compelling and valuable content, and see their page "likes" start to grow. The more interesting the content or engaging the brand, the faster the results came in. The rules were simple: Put out a great message, engage in conversations with your followers, offer promotions, and watch business expand both online and offline. However, these rules changed as Facebook expanded and felt pressure to show profits to its shareholders.

Books upon books, and even more blogs, detail how to get the most from a Facebook business page of all sizes and types. I will focus more on how to get results on an individual or personal basis. Just as using the network that we already have becomes easier once we are conscious of it, so does using the tools and the reach social media provides. Facebook is not exclusively the place for checking on friends and family or stalking exes. It can mobilize our social network to our cause, no matter how large or small that cause may be.

Most of what is covered going forward involves using the Facebook Page feature, although the tips also work for individual profile pages. The biggest difference is that Pages let the administrators track results, view engagement statistics, and pay for views, whereas regular profile pages do not. These benefits, along with a couple of others I will cover soon, make Pages useful for anyone wanting to build a personal brand or get more from the platform. I list a simple resource in the back of the book for those uncertain what a fan page is or for those who want to build one.[21] This resource, along with the rest of this chapter, will ensure initial success with your Facebook page.

Can You Post Too Much?

I was in a meeting for a local non-profit for which I volunteer. They were discussing social media and their Facebook strategy. They already have a great brand and are one of the most recognizable non-profits in the area. The problem with their social media performance was a lack of engagement. They were low on likes for the impact they have on the community, they were not posting regularly, and when they did post, they seldom had anything for the follower to do other than "like" the post. Someone at the table said, "We want to make sure we are not posting too much. We do not want to fill up people's feeds." I asked what they thought too much might be. They responded that they should only post a couple of times a week.

This comment struck me because, in researching and experimenting with Facebook, I know the reach is relatively low. On average, a typical post reaches about 16 percent of the total followers of the page, according to Facebook.[22]

Think about that. On average, only 16 percent. That means we could post up to six times a day and maybe reach 100 percent of our followers. That is a lot more posts than a couple of times per week.

I am not recommending individuals post that often unless they have the content and time to maintain fresh and engaging posts. Most individuals trying to build personal brands and increase their online presence will not have enough of either to ensure success.

The solution is to meet in the middle. I now only post when there is something truly valuable that the post is offering. These posts can be informative and full of information my audience may benefit from. They can be short videos explaining updates to the financial markets or new rules. Some are recaps of recent meetings or events I have attended that I found value in. Most posts also have a call to action.

Such calls to action are as simple as asking for a like or share or as complex as soliciting donations or captioning a picture for a contest. They give the reader something to do with the content. A good call to action increases user engagement and expands your reach to other circles of influence. Take your own Facebook feed, for example. It is continually filling up with posts your friends have either commented on or liked. This is why having a call to action is important—the more people like or comment on a post, the more people will eventually see it.

Another important component to increasing engagement on posts is the use of pictures and videos. Facebook's algorithms continually change, and more times than not, posts with pictures are seen by more followers than posts without. People love visuals. In the last several years, two newer platforms, Pinterest and Instagram, have used pictures almost exclusively to help individuals connect. The next time you go out to eat, look around the restaurant, and I guarantee you will see people taking pictures of their food. If you need further proof, check out Snapchat and TikTok. Both rely almost exclusively on short video content and have exploded both in popularity and usage in recent years. I am not suggesting you should start taking pictures of your food and posting selfies multiple times a day. Instead, I am suggesting that you include as many pictures or videos as make sense with your brand and message. If you are passionate about cooking, go ahead and post a picture of the delicacy you created. If you are passionate about fashion, by all means, post a picture of the latest trend you are setting. If you are passionate about volunteering, post a picture or video of you making a difference in someone's life. After all, a picture or a video has a far greater impact and reach than words alone.

The final suggestion for when and how to post is to experiment. Each page and audience is different. Depending on the content, one page may see more engagement on a Friday afternoon compared to one that sees a spike on Tuesday morning. Use the tools Facebook supplies and watch for spikes in activity. If you notice more users interact on Thursday afternoon, then make your most important posts on Thursday afternoon. There are no hard and fast rules as to when to post. It is up to you to figure out when your audience is most engaged and to use that time to make the biggest impact.

Be Interactive

The wonderful and equally terrifying thing about Facebook and social media is that it gives individuals an opportunity to have a voice they never had before. Anyone can post, comment, and message those they are connected to. This free flow of information allows for the exchange of ideas and for individuals to interact with brands like never before. People can share great experiences as easily as negative ones. It also means more responsibility lies with the person controlling the page to interact appropriately and in a timely manner no matter how positive or negative the interaction.

I started wearing bow ties on a whim in early 2012. Some friends thought it would be fun to tag me in photos on Facebook with them wearing bow ties, and one friend in particular, Zac Bales-Henry, randomly declared each Wednesday "Bow Tie Wednesday." His picture garnered over 150 likes in a relatively short amount of time, and I created my first ever Facebook page—"Bow Tie Wednesday"—later that afternoon. The goal? To encourage people of all backgrounds to wear bow ties on Wednesdays, just for fun.

We started to garner a following. It started with our own local friends and family members posting pictures of themselves in bow ties on Wednesday to our page. We'd like the photos, comment, occasionally share, and interact in any way we could. Soon pictures started to come in from the Midwest, then the coasts, then Canada, and shortly thereafter, all over the world. Men, women, kids, dogs, cats, all in bow ties on Wednesdays because of a random Facebook post and page created almost as an afterthought.

The engagement continued, and people started asking why we had created the page, what we wanted to do with it, and how they could help us do something bigger than just creating a page for bow tie lovers. Zac and I put our heads together and determined we could raise money for charity by hosting a "Bow Tie Ball" and encouraging people to purchase non-profit branded bow ties we designed. We ended up partnering with Variety, the Children's Charity, out of downtown Des Moines and held our first event in the fall of 2012. Over the next several years, the Bow Tie Ball grew, and we raised additional money all through online activity and engagement. We ended the event in 2016 after reaching our personal goal of raising a total of $100,000 for the organization.

People expect immediate interaction with social media. It is assumed that, because a page exists, someone is watching that page. Responding to questions and interacting with the audience needs the same attention as returning a text or answering an email. In some cases, it may require more attention. Doing so helps to build a good rapport with the audience and increase followers' visits and interaction on the page.

Interacting does not have to be complicated or time-consuming. Sometimes, it is as simple as liking a good comment or thanking someone for their insights. Other times, it will take a thought-out response or additional research. The most important thing to remember is that the page is not a one-way street. Information flows out of the page as easily as it does in. Using this information and responding appropriately can pay bigger dividends than just posting great content and can sometimes help raise money for kids who need it.

Should You Pay to Play?

Facebook developers keep making it easier to spend money on advertising to reach a target market or get more views. Once upon a time, the only return was an increase in page likes. This was done by taking out an advertisement and selecting demographics based on several options. The ad aimed as broad as "anyone over age 13 worldwide" to as specific as "37-year-old females in the 50266 zip code who speak French and are interested in auto racing." The more specific the demographic, the more money it cost per like. This option still exists, but others have been added.

The Facebook Ads Manager allows administrators to specify what they want their returns to be. The options include everything from gaining additional page likes to prompting clicks to obtaining event responses. In addition to advertising, there is also the option to boost an individual post and pay for additional views. Boosting a post forces it to appear in the timelines of followers and friends of followers. The more money spent on the boost, the more people will see the post.

But is it worth it? With the right planning, it can be. Using Facebook advertising is similar to being consistent with your content. Randomly spending 20 dollars here and 40 dollars there on ads with no real purpose will get you additional likes, but it seldom increases follower engagement. There must be a plan and a goal to make the most of your advertising dollars. Consider these questions before spending your hard-earned money:

1. Is my purpose for the ad to increase my total likes, or do I have another goal in mind?

2. Who is my target market? Do I want to reach a broad or specific market?

3. Am I putting out enough great content to actively engage new followers?

4. How will I determine if the ad is successful?

5. Do I have a long-term strategy, or am I experimenting for the short-term?

6. What is my monthly budget for ads?

These questions determine what your advertising strategy should be. Remember that the more specialized the audience, the more it will cost to reach each member. I encourage anyone who is new to Facebook's Pages to experiment with the ads before developing a full strategy. Put out random ads, and test the waters. Try combinations of pictures, videos, and calls to action. Use the available options, and become comfortable with them before spending a lot of money. Boost a post to see what effect, if any, it has on user engagement.

Running Facebook ads can be a great way to immediately impact your brand's reach. Ads should be part of a long-term marketing strategy in order to realize their full benefit. Put together that strategy, along with a monthly budget, and watch your audience grow. Continue to put out great content, and those new followers will become engaged followers.

Does It Actually Work?

My wife and I moved to Dallas Center, Iowa, in the summer of 2015. As we were going through the typical experience of turning on water and working with the local city government to ensure everything was transferred to our names, I discovered an opportunity in the form of a vacant city council seat. The city clerk and mayor encouraged me to apply for the open seat, and a month later, I was appointed to the Dallas Center City Council. Shortly after, I had to run in the November election to retain my seat.

I immediately set up a Facebook page—"Beyer for Dallas Center" and started posting information about myself, town events, and helpful reminders to community members. The page gained an audience relatively quickly, and I found myself interacting with people I had never formally met. Various individuals asked questions about meetings, road issues, and voiced their concerns. I responded as quickly and openly as I could, always encouraging additional dialog where appropriate. We had fruitful debates and simple clarifications of information. It felt good to be providing correct and relevant information to those wanting it.

Using the Facebook Ads Manager program, I was able to promote the new page for a relatively low cost to individuals 18+ years old in a ten-mile radius of the Dallas Center zip code. Additional followers liked the page, and my influence continued to grow. I set up specific posts with calls to action asking for people willing to display a yard sign or reminding people to mark their calendars for the upcoming vote. Some of these posts were boosted, and I tracked their performance compared to those that were allowed to grow organically. I noticed more people recognizing my family and me as we walked around town, visited the local ice cream shop, or played in the park. Many strangers came up to me, introduced themselves, and explained they knew who I was because of my Facebook presence. More often than not, they thanked me for putting out information they found useful. More than one person told me that I had their vote in the upcoming election.

My campaign continued, and I followed the basic rules of a local election. Continue to build a social media presence, send out mailers to frequent voters, get some yard signs out, and, above all—door knock. Through numerous articles and searches on Google, I determined that the key to my success would be actual face-to-face meetings and shaking hands through door-knocking.

I printed off additional fliers, got my list of voters, and committed to door-knocking on a cold mid-Saturday morning about a month before election day. The doorbell rang, and the first resident appeared on their porch. I explained who I was, why I was running, and asked for their vote.

"I've seen your Facebook page, and I got your letter. You got my vote, and feel free to stick a sign in my yard," was the response I received. The next two houses told me the same thing. After that, I was convinced I didn't need to continue knocking. Enough people had seen my messaging and appreciated what I was doing to provide value to the community.

Even though there were four people running for three open seats and one very active write-in campaign, I still received the most votes. At this point in time, my family and I had lived in the community for approximately three and a half months, and I still received more votes than anyone else running. To this day, I credit that initial win to the presence and the engagement I fostered through my Council Facebook page and the connections I was able to make through it.

In fact, I won my re-election bid to Council four years later in 2019 and was elected mayor in 2021 by a landslide, all without knocking on a single door. At the watch party the night of the results, the city clerk turned to me and said, "I never thought you'd be able to win an election by that margin without knocking on a single door. It's a different world out there."

It is indeed. Like it or not, when used correctly, social media, and specifically Facebook, can make connecting and expanding your influence easier than you ever dreamed.

Social Media Tips – Facebook

Good Facebook posts are short and typically contain a call to action. Posts with pictures or videos are set up to receive more traffic. Write down a short list of ideas or topics on which you can post and what your desired return or outcome (call to action) is with each post. Now go post!

1. Post idea:

_____

_____

_____

_____

_____

2. Call to action; desired outcome:

_____

_____

_____

_____

_____

3. Post idea:

_____

_____

_____

_____

_____

4. Call to action; desired outcome:

_____

_____

_____

_____

_____

CHAPTER 10

Networking with Twitter

Twitter was founded in 2006 and continues to grow to this day. Users in the United States make up roughly 10% of the 330 million monthly active users as of 2019. One of the more unique stats with this platform is that the top 10% of users generate 80% of the content on the platform. It's also utilized primarily by those ranging in age from 25-49 or mostly "millennials" as they're traditionally defined. As of 2020, Twitter has 35 million daily users of the platform.[23] Yet despite all of the active users and shared data, the most frequently asked questions I hear are, "What does Twitter really do?" or "What is the point of Twitter?"

The great thing about Twitter is that it can be whatever the user wants it to be. It can be a place for users to tweet opinions or chat with friends. It can be a place where individuals follow their favorite stores or brands or keep up-to-date on issues they care about. It can be a place to expand influence and create content. It can also be a venue for directing traffic to blogs or websites. Twitter offers these things and more due to its simple functionality and ease of use. It literally allows users to follow any person, brand, or idea and interact directly with the person on the other side of that account. That is the power of Twitter.

What are people doing on Twitter? An article posted in March 2022 on *The Teal Mango* platform uncovered interesting trends in what users are currently doing on Twitter. Some striking facts include:

- More than 575,000 tweets are sent out each minute
- 83% of world leaders use Twitter
- $70 million was spent on Twitter ads in 2017
- 66% of US companies with over 100 employees use Twitter for marketing
- On average, a Twitter user follows around 5–6 businesses
- 60% of users expect brands to respond to their tweet within one hour
- Globally, men use Twitter more than women[24]

Twitter is a great resource to share and create content while spreading influence. When used correctly, it helps cement a personal brand and allows for one-on-one interaction that most other social media platforms lack. Twitter gives a larger voice to its users because it currently provides more visible content compared to the way Facebook algorithms filter content based on your previous usage. This sheer amount of unfiltered content tends to overwhelm new users. Going forward, I will discuss how to get past content overload and use Twitter to expand your network and influence.

Whom to Follow?

I was presenting a personal branding keynote to a group of college students when a woman in the back raised her hand and told me, "Twitter is useless because everyone is always talking about where they went to eat or who they are dating. No one says anything of value, which is why I will never be on Twitter." I smiled politely and told her I agreed with some of what she was saying. There is a lot of garbage on Twitter. People are tweeting random information that has little to no value for followers. We continued our discussion that it also gives a voice to people who traditionally didn't have one. Everyone from your neighbor to a famous sports athlete or movie celebrity can now give you insight into what they're thinking or the contents of their daily routine. There can be some great information shared, but there can also be a lot of wasted space. "So, what do I do if I want to use it for the great information, she asked?" I told her the easiest way to solve that problem was to be selective on whom she followed.

Finding the right people or brands to follow is one of the

most asked questions I hear when I talk about Twitter. It seems to mystify many people. To get more out of your Twitter experience, follow the people or companies that provide the information you want. The platform offers various methods for finding these individuals. You can search by name or handle (username). A Google search including the keyword "Twitter" and name of the person or brand will show you their Twitter information. You can search based on your interests. Twitter itself provides recommendations to follow based on who you currently follow, and most of your favorite brands have a presence on Twitter. You can even see who your favorite accounts follow by going through the list of accounts they follow.

Twitter makes it easy to find new and interesting people by giving users access to who other users are following. I love browsing through followers, lists, and favorites of the users who provide the best content. These lists are built-in tracking mechanisms that Twitter provides, so users can easily access past information. I usually end up finding better information from those lists than through searches because the users I follow have already vetted others.

Finding great people to follow on Twitter need not be time-consuming or involve tremendous thought. It can simply mean finding one influencer on your passions and then following ten accounts that influencer follows. Use the built-in connectivity Twitter provides to increase the value of the content in your stream, and watch as the garbage posts disappear.

One of my favorite things to do with Twitter in 2022 is

follow Iowa State athletics. It's no secret that I'm a huge Iowa State fan, and the connectivity and network Twitter provides are incredible. I've been able to connect with fellow Iowa State fans, alumni, players, coaches, broadcasters, and staff all through Twitter. Replying to tweets, congratulating players, and watching fellow fans' reactions are some of my favorite things to do during football or basketball games. It helps relieve the stress that being an Iowa State fan often causes and allows for a shared community in both victory and defeat. Sure, it may not help me with business development, but it's a lot of fun, and sometimes that's just as important.

The Power of the

The hashtag is one of the most useful and, sometimes, most annoying features of Twitter. It is useful because it creates a searchable database within the platform. To create a hashtag, the user puts a # symbol before a word or phrase, which generates a link. Clicking this link shows all other tweets marked with that hashtag. Most TV shows, live events, and several companies include hashtags in their advertising. The hashtag is an easy-to-use and valuable tool for connecting.

Hashtags can be annoying when they are overused, as Justin Timberlake and Jimmy Fallon point out in their YouTube video "#Hashtag."[25] The point of the hashtag is to make relevant, useful information easier to find, so users can share ideas and connect with one another. Hashtags allow users to separate valuable content from the noise that can make up one's Twitter feed.

Here are some effective ways I have used hashtags on Twitter:

1. I do not make up my own hashtags unless I want to specifically track something personal.

2. Twitter auto fills trending or common hashtags after typing a few letters, much like Google does during a search. Use these autofill suggestions to see greater engagement with your tweets.

3. I do not use more than three hashtags in a single tweet. After three hashtags, the message gets watered down and less relevant in searches.

4. Use hashtags wisely by keeping them on topic with your tweets. I tweeted as I was working on this book and always included the hashtag #author. I have gained over 100 new followers thanks to this hashtag alone. People want to connect with other users who share their interests. Help them find you.

5. Try live tweeting during an event using the assigned hashtag for that event. Every major sporting event, live show, television series, and marketing campaign provides a hashtag. Find the hashtag associated with something you are passionate about and read what other people are saying.

A big part of using Twitter effectively and building a

strong brand lies in correctly using hashtags. They are a valuable tool for building credibility and recognition in a content-heavy environment. Experiment and spend time looking for hashtags that provide you with the best information. Twitter will become a more enjoyable experience when you connect with the right people who share the information you want.

Creating Versus Filtering Content

I joined Twitter in April 2011. My first years using it were spent watching my feed. I followed all kinds of users: local influencers, brands, celebrities, and companies. Twitter kept me up on current trends, and I occasionally voiced my opinion on those trends. That did little for my personal branding or my influence because I was not sure what my voice should be. I did not know what content to share or what to say because I was overwhelmed by the continual data and content filling my feed. I read multiple articles emphasizing the importance of tweeting eight, twelve, or twenty-plus times a day to get results. I knew I would never devote the time needed to produce that much content, and I did not want to waste my time without seeing results. So, I continued to watch what others were doing, and my profile sat dormant.

In early 2014, an article in my LinkedIn feed changed that. The title struck me instantly: "How to spend only 10 minutes per day on Twitter." I could not help but click the link. The article changed how I approached Twitter overnight. In it, Aubre Andrus explained that by organizing important connections, we can funnel the most important content into easy-to-follow lists that vastly increase the platform's efficiency. Furthermore, she explained how the hashtag (#, formerly known as the pound sign) and other Twitter features work. She also introduced me to third-party applications, such as Hootsuite, which allow users to be active on Twitter without having to be on Twitter constantly.

Following her tips, I immediately saw results as my followers increased as well as the number of retweets and favorites I received. This led to an exciting breakthrough. Interaction increased as well. I started setting appointments through Twitter and receiving direct messages from people interested in me and my product. Entire conversations took place as they would if I was texting someone. Both my business and my influence expanded. People started coming to me for advice on using Twitter because I was now organized and using the platform successfully.

The best part of the experience was that I was not creating a ton of original content. I became a content filterer more than a content creator, and my followers appreciated that. A content filterer, by my definition, is a user who reads a lot of content and filters out the best information through either retweets or favorites. This allowed me to not only expand my knowledge but also expand my brand. Filtering content is an easy way to become an influencer without always developing great, original content. An added benefit of content filtering is that the users I follow appreciate the retweets and the interaction I provide. It allows them to expand their influence through exposure to my followers and allows me to provide value.

Creating original content on Twitter takes more finessing

than on Facebook due to the character limitation, but it can be done. When using Twitter to create content, I typically tweet a teaser with a call to action requiring the user to click a link. I experience a higher click-through rate on Twitter than Facebook, typically between three to five percent. Twitter is the driving factor of traffic to my blog and website due to the interaction and value I offer my followers.

Remember that by taking time and getting organized, anyone can be on Twitter and not let it consume their life. Using the list feature and following individuals who provide great content will make it easy to filter that content to your followers, which may inspire you to create your own. Do not let the constant influx of information on your Twitter feed overwhelm you. Instead, embrace it and use it to your advantage. Share valuable content, create your own, and watch your followers (and influence) grow.

Message Anyone

Twitter separates itself from the other platforms because of its total openness. Open accounts allow anyone who also has an open account to follow and interact with them. It allows NFL fans to tweet to their favorite players and occasionally get a response. It allows movie fans to tweet to their favorite actors and give them feedback on films. It allows individuals to critique or compliment their favorite restaurants directly to those restaurants. Do not be afraid to use this feature.

So many options exist to communicate today that getting in front of someone can be tricky. I found that when phone calls are not returned or emails are unanswered, a tweet often gets a response. Twitter is far less formal than traditional communication methods, and people let their guard down for a tweet more readily than an email. Just as a Houston Texans' cheerleader agreed to go to prom with a kid who direct messaged her through Twitter, so may a person agree to have coffee with you who has not responded to any other communication.[27]

The next time you find yourself at a loss trying to reach someone, look for their Twitter account. Research what the person tweets and find a common interest. Send the person a message or reply to a tweet to establish common ground. Express your desire to get to know the person better and ask for a meeting. The worst the person can say is no. However, you may be pleasantly surprised how often you hear yes.

Twitter is only an overwhelming funnel of useless information if you let it be. Follow accounts that spread great content. Organize those accounts into strategic lists and engage with those users. Share their content and create your own. Do not be afraid to use the openness that Twitter offers by messaging individuals you want to know better.

Social Media Tips—Twitter

Hashtags are a quick and easy reference point to find great information and get noticed. A quick Google search such as "hashtags for restaurants" turns up dozens of articles and suggestions for popular hashtags involving restaurants. Do some research and figure out what hashtags are being used by your industry or your interest. Record them below and figure out how to include them in some of your tweets going forward.

1. Popular industry hashtags:

_____

_____

_____

_____

2. Hobbies or interests hashtags:

_____

_____

_____

_____

Connecting with the right people on Twitter makes the platform much more interactive and beneficial. Take a moment and write a short list of influential people you would like to connect with on Twitter. These can be actors or actresses, comedians, political figures, authors, speakers, chefs, athletes, community leaders, CEOs, or countless others. Google "Twitter handle" and the person's name to see if they're on Twitter, and then follow them for updates!

1. Top 10 people I want to follow on Twitter:

_____

_____

_____

_____

CHAPTER 11

Networking with LinkedIn

Since the first edition of this book, LinkedIn has grown by leaps and bounds and has passed Twitter in terms of total users. As of the end of 2021, the platform had nearly 800 million users worldwide and is home to over 55 million companies.[28] I still believe that of the three platforms mentioned in this book, LinkedIn is the most useful for expanding influence, growing a personal brand, and making things happen in the real and digital worlds. In the spirit of full disclosure, I am incredibly biased toward LinkedIn because it has, and continues, to help me achieve more than the other two platforms combined.

LinkedIn was founded in 2002 and has grown into one of the web's most significant tools for employers and employees to share information. Once the ground of recruiters and IT professionals, LinkedIn became more open and accepted among all generations as a viable tool to connect with other professionals. Forty percent of users check their accounts at least once daily. Thirteen percent update their profiles daily. As of late 2021, LinkedIn claimed it could help users connect or reach up to 65 million decision-makers. Perhaps even more interesting is the fact that 55% of those decision-makers use content they find on LinkedIn to determine which organizations to work with.[29] While Facebook and Twitter allow anyone to have a social or personal presence, LinkedIn allows a professional presence, and this cannot be ignored.

LinkedIn seems to confuse many people. They do not understand the purpose of the platform other than having an online resume. I've been asked more than once, "But won't my company think I'm looking for a job?" or, "I don't want to get fired because my boss sees I'm connected with a competitor or vendor on LinkedIn." It seems that more individuals are creating accounts exclusively when they are looking for a job versus using it for all of the tools it offers. Frankly, most senior executives I know or have talked to expect their employees to be on LinkedIn whether they're happily employed or not. They understand that an online presence is an integral part of society today. If you don't already have a profile established, I hope that you'll finish this section and set one up today!

Keep in mind that there is much more to LinkedIn than

putting out a good headshot and a lofty resume. It is no longer a platform for elite professionals. Industry leaders create thousands of topics and fantastic content through LinkedIn. This, coupled with the availability to create in-person relationships through the platform, makes it essential to expanding one's network and brand.

The following insights will help you see immediate results from the resources LinkedIn provides. I will help you discover how to utilize the platform to find content and insights you care about. I explore how to turn digital connections into face-to-face connections. I also look at how LinkedIn's content-creating features help almost anyone become an influencer and experience a greater flow of online traffic. By implementing these tips, I show how easy it is to turn LinkedIn into a networking supersite.

Great Content

A lot has changed with the algorithm and information featured on LinkedIn since the first edition of this book was published. Originally called "The Pulse of the Industry," this section once covered how LinkedIn integrated a search feature called "Pulse" that let users discover content that directly impacted their professional careers or they simply found interesting. As is the current trend in most social platforms, less is more, and that separate feature has now been integrated into the usability of LinkedIn. It's still incredibly easy to find influencers, brands, and content you care about; it's simply changed a little.

The fastest way to find what you're looking for on LinkedIn is to use the search bar. What was once used solely to find people can now be used to find everything the site has to offer. Sure, it still has a tilt toward people as that is what the platform was originally created for, but you can use it to find companies, content, thought leaders, and more. Interested in a specific company and what openings they may have? Type the company name in the search bar; chances are they have a profile. Curious what people are posting about in regards to a passion or hobby you have? Type in those keywords, and LinkedIn will give you the option to see posts from people talking about those criteria and much more. Want to connect with someone who is a project manager or marketing executive? Type in those keywords, and LinkedIn will show you who you may be indirectly connected to.

But what happens if you don't know what to search for or how to find companies that do what you're interested in? Check out the left side of the page under your profile, and you'll see an option that says, "Discover more." Click this link to see a whole list of people, companies, and content that LinkedIn has self-selected based on your interactions with the platform and what they think might interest you. I've managed to find some great new connections, follow industry leaders who are providing insights not seen in other sources, and even move business forward using these recommended connections.

Speaking of connections...

Should I Connect with You?

Numerous times, I have either sent or received a blind connection request. These requests are sent when no prior relationship exists. Sometimes, they are people I want to connect with or struggle to contact. Sometimes, they are influencers in the community I want to get to know. Sometimes, I just like their profiles and find them interesting. Blind requests are one of the things I get questioned about the most regarding LinkedIn.

The question of connecting with someone you do not know is interesting because it depends on how people want to use the platform. Many salespeople connect with anyone who sends a request because the more people they are connected to, the better. People in other careers are often more selective, usually only connecting with established relationships. To decide whom you should and should not connect with, figure out what you want the platform to do for you. Determine whether you want to keep your connections intimate or if you want to expand your influence and take a chance on individuals you do not know. Set some basic rules for how to deal with blind connections when they do come in.

My first rule is to always connect with anyone within driving distance. If I can drive to you in less than a day, I will connect with you. By being within driving distance, I may get to meet you face-to-face. My second rule is to connect with anyone I find interesting after viewing his or her profile. If we have common hobbies, I connect. If we work in the same industry, I connect. If we studied the same things in school, I connect. My final rule is to try to meet all blind connections face-to-face at least once after we connect.

I like the final rule because it is another step in building real relationships instead of relying on online ones. I also like it because I am rarely turned down when I request a meeting after accepting a connection. These meeting requests are made right in the LinkedIn messaging service, and I use the same dialog each time I set one up. "Thank you so much for connecting with me on LinkedIn. I noticed we have (specific detail) in common, and I would love to get together to learn more about you. Are you available for coffee next week?" This approach has led to long-term, beneficial relationships with people I may not have otherwise met.

The next time a blind connection comes through in your inbox, take a second before deleting it and go into the individual's page. There is a reason they sent you a request. Maybe it is to sell you something or to expand the number of connections they have. More often than not though, the requests are made for nobler reasons. Instead of denying the request, figure out if the stranger on the other end offers value. Schedule a meeting and turn that blind connection into an actual connection. You may be surprised by the results.

LinkedIn Socials

In the winter of 2012, a close friend, Mike Banasiak, ran an idea by me. He was frustrated with LinkedIn because he was not seeing results and could not figure out how to make the platform work for him. He wanted to find a way to turn his "weak online connections into strong, real-life connec-tions." His idea: bring together two to three super-connected individuals and host a "LinkedIn Social." The socials would be held at various locations around the Greater Des Moines area with one goal in mind: to encourage our LinkedIn connections to meet face-to-face and build real relationships. I asked where I could sign up.

A few short months later, we held our first social at a local winery. We sent out LinkedIn messages to all of our Des Moines area connections and invited them to the winery on a specific date and time. Food and drinks were covered by sponsors and by us as hosts. There were no sales pitches and no programs, just face-to-face networking that allowed our connections to meet us and each other in a low-pressure, friendly environment. That first event drew 65 attendees, which was amazing considering it happened in Iowa in February in the middle of a snowstorm. The next morning, my LinkedIn feed was filled with updates about individuals connecting who had met each other at our social. We knew we were onto something.

Since that first event, numerous others have drawn anywhere from 100 to 250 people, many of whom have never attended a networking event. I have met with dozens of indi-viduals thanks to these events and have seen my personal brand grow in the community. The socials accomplished what Mike set out for them to do: they allowed attendees to turn weak online connections into strong real-life connections.

I am not suggesting that the best way to get the most out of your LinkedIn account is to have a big networking party and invite all your connections to food and drinks on your dime. I am suggesting these socials prove that many online connections want to build personal relationships. In fact, we discontinued the socials in 2018 after LinkedIn made it harder to export our contact lists and get the word out. However, I continue to connect and have meetings with new connections on a regular basis, thanks to the doors those original socials opened.

The simplest way to connect with individuals through LinkedIn is the messaging service, which is a lot like sending a direct message on Twitter or Facebook. It allows individuals to send messages to any of their connections and, if it is a paid account, to users with whom they are not connected. Like Twitter, this messaging service holds more clout than phone calls and emails. In my experience, I always have a LinkedIn message returned unless the connection's contact information is outdated. In general, people pay more attention when the message they receive is from LinkedIn instead of from an ordinary email account.

I recommend to all active LinkedIn users to try the messaging service and request an appointment with a connection they want to know better. Building a useful network on LinkedIn is dependent on having real relationships with the individuals you are connected to. Get out from behind the computer screen and meet face-to-face. Go to a coffee shop or have a beer after work. Talk about their interests and yours and turn that weak online connection into something valuable: a real-life relationship.

The "Write" Stuff

Another huge evolution of the LinkedIn platform was the addition of new and expanded content creation tools. For many years LinkedIn fell behind Facebook and, to a lesser extent, Twitter on how and what content was allowed on the platform. It was seen as a professional platform and didn't allow the freedom to post videos or extended written posts. Fortunately, that has changed for the better.

LinkedIn now offers all of the same features that the most popular social media platforms offer. You can write content, share photos, and post videos with only a few short clicks. While this is great because of the number of options it provides, it can also be a little overwhelming. So, which one is best?

The short answer is whichever one you prefer. I've personally tested all three methods and have had consistent and positive results with each. Again, the most important component ends being the medium that allows you to be consistent with your message and gives you the ability to share great content, no matter what form that content ends up taking. If you prefer writing blogs or short posts to convey your ideas, do it. If you're better at videos and have a passion for recording yourself or others, take that route. Maybe you're a photographer, or photography is an integral part of what you're passionate about. Share those pictures and encourage your network to check them out. There are some tricks and tips to getting additional views and interactions with your posts no matter what form they take.

One of the biggest drivers of engagement on LinkedIn is the comment feature. LinkedIn likes interaction between users and gives a weighted advantage to those posts that have comments. The easiest way to get people to comment is to simply ask them to. Ask for their opinion on your article or picture. Ask them what they think or if they want more information at the conclusion of your video. The more specific you can be with your questioning, the more likely you are to get actual feedback on the post.

As I said, LinkedIn likes interaction between users. The next step is to reply to the comments you're receiving. Thank people for their thoughts or continue the discussion if they make a good point. This back and forth encourages additional interaction from other users and gets your post more visibility to connections through the LinkedIn algorithm.

Some other easy but not as effective tools are the use of hashtags in posts and getting "likes" or other reactions. Like Twitter, the use of hashtags to help connections find your posts has dramatically increased in recent years. Try mixing and matching various hashtags that are pertinent to your topic to see what kind of engagement they bring. Look at other users, especially influencers, to see what hashtags they commonly use and implement them as part of your strategy. Encourage people to like your posts, and you'll start to see your engagement multiply.

The other side of the coin is engaging with others on LinkedIn. Don't just expect people to interact with you if you're not taking a little time to like, comment, or interact with their posts. As we talked about previously, people are reciprocal by nature. Try taking an interest in some of the connections you have, and you'll be surprised with how quickly they return the favor.

Social Media Tips – LinkedIn

LinkedIn is one of the most underutilized platforms. Most people believe it's only beneficial when they're looking for a new job, but it has so much more potential! The ability to connect with influencers and find great content is unlimited.

• Log onto your account and click on the "Discover More" link for a list of industries, influencers, and topics to follow. Pick at least three influencers that interest you as well as five to ten industries or topics. This will help round out your newsfeed and give you great content to start sharing. Record who and what you followed:

_____

_____

_____

_____

The messaging service on LinkedIn is given more credibility than most other forms of communication by active users. Use this system to set appointments with individuals you would like to get to know better.

• Go through your connections and write down at least three people you would like to meet face-to-face. Reach out and set an appointment through the LinkedIn messaging tool.

_____

_____

_____

_____

Other tips:

1. Most people don't receive updates from LinkedIn because they don't have a current email address in the system. Login to your account and double-check that your email is one that you check regularly.

2. Have a professional headshot for your profile pictures. LinkedIn is the most professional of the social media platforms. Having a great profile picture that is easily recognizable makes a better first impression.

3. Share information and post regularly. Cross-post from Twitter and Facebook if you already have professional posts on those platforms.

CHAPTER 12

Networking in the Digital Age

So much has changed since March of 2020. My last meeting prior to the world shutting down was with a friend and client at Olive Garden in West Des Moines (had I known it was going to be the last in-restaurant dining experience I was going to have in a long time, I would have chosen somewhere local). We talked about everything going on and if the state would even shut down. Surely it wouldn't, but if it had to, we could all handle the two weeks it would take to flatten the curve.

Up to that point in my life, my career and much of my social life relied on seeing people in person. My business development relied on meeting people at their offices or over coffee or drinks. After I got over the initial shock of being in the middle of a global pandemic and what that meant for my family and friends, it hit me that I didn't know the first thing about maintaining, let alone building, my network without in-person interactions. I was lost and a little afraid.

I'd be lying if I said that I slept on it one night and then jumped right into the new world of digital and online networking. My online presence and brand were already built, but, as I stated above, I used it to meet with people face-to-face, not through Zoom. Once the initial shock wore off that in-person meetings were simply not going to be an option for a long time, I did what it seemed like everyone else in the world was doing. I went even more online.

It started with online client meetings and reviews. Next came networking groups and Zoom happy hours with friends. I quickly realized that even though human contact was no longer available, and I wouldn't be shaking anyone's hand for a while, relationships could still be built and maintained online, just like I had been doing for years in person. In fact, some of the interactions and relationship maintenance activities were made easier online. No more small talk about the weather, no more disingenuous communication, just meaningful messages and shared empathy given the situation we all found ourselves in.

As the pandemic continued, it became clear that people were going to adopt this new form of online communication for years to come. I joke now that if nothing else, the pandemic moved our utilization of online tools at least ten years into the future in a matter of months. Business started to flow again, and our Zoom happy hours started getting themes. Then my phone began to ring with businesses, entrepreneurs, and non-profits looking for ways to network when in-person meetings weren't happening. It dawned on me that there was a brand new way to network that was now acceptable and removed the limits that most in-person meetings entailed. We no longer had to worry about distance keeping us from meeting with new people or even time constraints as meetings could be booked up to the minute. By closing down the world, a new one had opened.

The More Things Change, the More They Stay the Same

Over the course of 2020 and 2021, I gave at least two dozen networking presentations and keynote speeches to groups of all sizes. Some were 100% digital; others were hybrid, and, towards the end of 2021, a lot became 100% in-person again. Some general themes seemed to emerge, most of which have already been covered by previous chapters in this book. Questions such as:

"How do I build a relationship through Zoom with someone I've never met?"

"What do I talk about?"

"Are there certain rules of etiquette that should be followed or best practices I can learn from?"

And my personal favorite, *"How do I follow up or keep the relationship going?"*

If you've been reading in chapter order, you'll likely already be able to answer some of the questions above. If you skipped right to this section, answers to these questions can be found in previous chapters, but here's a quick recap of how I answered these questions in the digital age of networking.

"How do I build a relationship with someone I've never met through Zoom?"

The simplest way to build a new relationship goes back to asking better questions. A lot of the same questions can be asked through a computer screen just as easily as they can be asked in person. To this day, I still use the question "What's your story?" with most new acquaintances, no matter the environment in which we're meeting. It's a better question that allows the person I'm connecting with to share details about who they are, what they love, and their own personal history without forcing them to talk about work or make general small talk. It's a great question that allows for real communication to take place and a relationship to build.

The other key point is to make sure you listen to the answers. Don't allow yourself to become distracted by your phone or another tab on your computer screen. Shut down the email, log out of your social media, put your phone away, and give this person your undivided attention just as you would in a coffee shop or your office. Just because you're not physically with them doesn't mean you can allow your mind to wander. Plus, most people aren't as good at feigning attention as they think they are. Yes, we can tell you're looking at your phone or reading an email. Turn them off and be present with the person you're meeting.

"What do I talk about?"

Like the previous question, a lot of this goes back to asking better questions and then listening for where the conversation goes. Remember that people want to be heard, and if you're willing to listen, it's much easier to build a lasting connection.

Other topics can include, but are not limited to, hobbies, family, travel, favorite restaurants, books you're reading, and so on. I do enjoy taking a look at the background environment of the person I'm connecting with online to get a better sense of who they are or what they're interested in. I liken it to the first meeting at a prospect's office. Most people will display things they are proud of or interest them. The work from home movement has people allowing a deeper insight into their personal lives by having conversations in home offices, kitchens, dens, and living rooms. Take a quick look at the bookshelf or wall behind the person you're meeting with, and don't be afraid to ask about shared interests you may see.

"Are there certain rules of etiquette that should be followed or best practices I can learn from?"

Believe it or not, the basic rules we covered way back at the beginning of the book are just as applicable to digital networking as they are to in-person networking. We've already touched on some of them, including turning off distractions and being present with the person you're connecting with. Some other basics include making sure your background screen shows what you want it to and matches the brand you're trying to create. Be conscious of what the diploma, books, posters, artwork, or collectibles in your background tell the person you're meeting with about you. Does your background say, "I'm a professional looking to work with others," or does it give an "I'm only doing this because I need a paycheck" vibe?

Another key factor to consider is the sound and lighting you're using. I'm not going to recommend spending hundreds of dollars on a light bar and microphone. In fact, most computers and smartphones have built-in capabilities to ensure you have a professional appearance, but it's still good to ensure that the overhead light in your office or the setting sun in your west-facing room isn't creating an unwanted glare.

The final tip on best practices is to make sure you understand the technology that is being used and, if it's something new you haven't used before, try to test it prior to the meeting. Teams, GoToMeeting, Google Meets, and, to a lesser extent, FaceTime all have their strengths, and each one works a little differently. Some require online software downloads in order to operate, while others work solely in the cloud. It's one thing to show up to a meeting late because you're simply running late. It's another to show up late because you're frazzled and frustrated with a platform you haven't had experience with, and now you have to regather your thoughts and mindset for the meeting. And yes, I'm completely talking from experience on this one.

"How do I follow up or keep the relationship going?"

By far, the most asked question I receive is this one—*"How do I follow up?"* or *"How do I keep in touch?"*

Much of what was covered in Chapter 7, "Don't Forget About Me" still holds true to networking in the digital age. Maintaining and creating a follow-up routine is crucial to keeping a new relationship growing while also making sure existing relationships aren't forgotten. One of the true blessings of online meetings is the ability to connect with a large number of people in a much shorter amount of time. No more commute or drive time means meetings can happen without delays. As more and more people have grown accustomed to and comfortable with online meetings, the ability to communicate and stay in touch has also become easier, which means so has the ability to follow up and maintain those relationships.

This comfort has been the biggest change in my communication style. Messages that used to say, "Let me know when we can get together for coffee or a drink," now read, "Let me know if you're available for a Zoom meeting or if you prefer in person." I let the other person decide what they're most comfortable with, and then I accommodate their needs. I've found that this often creates an easier flow of dialogue and can save me time if the online option is chosen. If I'm personally pressed for time but know the meeting is important, I'll only offer the Zoom option, something that was completely unthinkable just a short time ago.

Whether you decide to put a spreadsheet in place, use a Customer Relationship Management (CRM) system provided by your employer, organize relationships by buckets, or simply rely on "Divine Intervention" to remind you when to reach out, one of the most important things to remember is don't overcomplicate it.

One of the things I see most people struggle with is putting in too many rules or creating so much busy work that they never actually do the reach-out or follow-up to continue building the relationship. More time goes by because the original reach-out was put off in favor of updating a worksheet or doing data entry in the CRM. Suddenly, the well-intentioned reach out in a timely manner is pushed off, and six months or more have gone by. It gets harder to reach out because so much time has gone by, and it doesn't seem as genuine as it once did. More time goes by, follow-ups aren't done, and another prospective relationship dies on the vine. Don't wait, and don't push the reach-out or follow-up. Just do it and move on to the next one.

These questions, and others, continue to come up as I present on what it's like to network in the digital age. As this section title alluded to, yes, things have changed, but despite those changes, a lot has stayed the same. People still want to connect and meet with others who have a genuine interest in them. It's easier to have a meaningful conversation if great questions are asked and listening takes place. Give those you're meeting with your undivided attention, and don't get distracted by other screens. Despite what others may tell you, or you may tell yourself, there is no magic formula or one perfect way to do follow-ups or keep in touch with your expanding network. Do what feels best to you and take action. It's better to send a follow-up message than to wonder what could have been. And remember, the more things change, the more they really stay the same.

Priorities

One of the blessings and, at the same time, a curse of networking in the digital age is the sheer amount of connectivity we all now possess. The "great resignation" has forced businesses to rethink how they manage their employees where flexibility and work-life balance now take priority over compensation and the opportunities for professional growth, according to a study by Ipsos.[30] People now have the ability to work virtually anywhere and at any time. While that may sound like an idyllic utopia to some, it comes with new pressures we're only now starting to understand.

Which brings me to the title of this section—Priorities. A few years ago, a friend of mine asked me if I was going to attend a chamber event that was held after hours. The exact time or purpose of the event doesn't matter. What mattered to me at the time was the fact that the event happened during what I had deemed "family time" in my house. This was time that I had promised my wife and daughters I would be home and would specifically not fill with work or networking events.

My friend told me that it surprised him. In his mind, I was going all of the time and networking whenever the opportunity presented itself. There was a time in my life, prior to having a family, when that may have been true. In fact, I actually pushed that lifestyle a little longer than I should have. It wasn't until my wife commented at dinner one night that it was "nice to finally have me home." Her words caught me off guard as it hadn't dawned on me that I hadn't been home at all that week due to work and networking engagements. We had a very transparent discussion, and she confessed that she missed having me around, and so did the girls. I committed to her that evening that I would work to reprioritize my obligations to her and to work.

I share this because, in our new, ultra-connected world, it's very easy to overcommit and over-schedule yourself. The saying "do you control your calendar, or does your calendar control you?" is one that I frequently remind myself of when life gets hectic. It was easy when I was younger and didn't have obligations at home to pack my calendar with happy hours and charity events. As my life changed, my priorities changed, and I had to give myself permission to turn down invitations or only commit after I checked both my work and family calendars. I'm glad I did.

Guard your time and your priorities as you build your network. You may find a time when you have to turn someone down because you know it's best for your own mental or physical health. Don't be afraid to tell them that you'd love to get together, but now isn't the best time, and stick to it. If there is one thing we could all continue to learn, it's the ability to say "no" and to slow down. Sure, we may have more flexibility in the workplace than we've ever had before. But is it really worth it if you just end up filling your calendar with more work?

CHAPTER 13

Conclusion

When talking with organizations, be it young professionals, small businesses, non-profits, or schools, I always ask, "By a show of hands, how many of you like networking?" Without fail, the majority keep their hands down. I ask someone with their hands under the table to give me a definition of networking. Inevitably, the response involves fear, a vague description of something done in the business world to get sales, or a negative definition of a structured event where people are forced to talk to one another when they would rather be doing something else. These answers are the reason I wrote this book.

Networking is a basic human need. We need relationships, and networking is one way to build those relationships. We all enjoy networking to varying degrees. We just need to realize that networking does not always have to center around sales, business, or structured events. Networking happens all around us all of the time on social media and through face-to-face interactions. Networking is the way people get things done professionally and personally.

The saying "one person can change the world" is still true as long as that person has a powerful network to help. We all have networks of friends and professionals willing to help us succeed. It is up to us to make those networks work. Do not be afraid to tell people what you want, and always be willing to help others. Develop a genuine interest in people and find their stories. We all have something interesting to say if we can find someone who will listen. Use the tools that social media provides to expand your influence, customize an online brand, and grow your network. In the digital age, connect where people are most comfortable and make use of the adaptation of technology. Through it all, be sure to guard your time and keep your priorities in check.

Networking does not have to be an exclusive, scary thing for professionals in suits to use to get ahead. It can benefit the non-profit as much as the for-profit. It can benefit your personal life as much as your professional life. If you are new to networking, get out of the car and attend that first event. If you are a seasoned professional, share your success and help others feel comfortable. Now, more than ever, we all must build our relationships and strengthen our ties.

NOTES

[1] www.dannybeyer.com

[2] Landa, S., & Duschinsky, R. (2013) "Crittenden's dynamic–maturational model of attachment and adaptation." *Review of General Psychology* 17.3

[3] Maslow, A. (1943). A theory of human motivation. *Psychological Review*, 50(4), 370-396

[4] The parent company of Facebook rebranded in 2021 and changed its name to Meta. However, as of the date of this writing, the social media platform continues to be referred to as Facebook.

[5]Croston, G. (2012, November 28). The thing we fear more than death. *Psychology Today*. Retrieved May 15, 2014, from http://www.psychologytoday.com/blog/the-real-story-risk/201211/the-thing-we-fear-more-death

[6]Carnegie, D. (1981). *How to win friends and influence people* (Rev. ed.). New York: Simon & Schuster, Inc.

[7]Adams, S. (2012, May 18). New survey: Majority of Employees dissatisfied. *Forbes*. Retrieved May 15, 2014, from http://www.forbes.com/sites/susanadams/2012/05/18/new-survey-majority-of-employees-dissatisfied/

[8]Tsung, F. (2014, February 27). Are business cards still relevant? *Entrepreneur*. Retrieved May 16, 2014, from http://www.entrepreneur.com/article/231811

[9]Marsden, P. (2013, November 14). Fast facts: Information overload 2013. *Digital Intelligence Today*. Retrieved May 16, 2014, from http://digitalintelligencetoday.com/fast-facts-information-overload-2013/

[10]Turk, G. (2014, April 25). *Look Up*. YouTube. Retrieved June 10, 2014, from http://www.youtube.com/watch?v=Z7dLU6fk9QY&feature=youtu.be

[11]Chorost, M. (2011). *World wide mind: The coming integration of humanity, machines and the Internet*. New York: Free Press.

[12]Spiegel, A. (2012, November 26). *Give and take: How the rule of reciprocation binds us*. NPR. Retrieved July 6, 2014, from http://www.npr.org/blogs/health/2012/11/26/165570502/give-and-take-how-the-rule-of-reciprocation-binds-us

[13]New-York Tribune. (New York [N.Y.]) 1866-1924, September 22, 1918, Page 9, Image 9. (1918, September 22). Retrieved October 25, 2014, from http://chroniclingamerica.loc.gov/lccn/ sn83030214/1918-09-22/ed-1/seq-9/

[14]Winfrey, G. (2014, July 14). The most powerful people in your network who you're not tapping. *Inc.com*. Retrieved July 21, 2014, from http://www.inc.com/graham-winfrey/networking-tips-from-whartons-adam-grant.html?cid=sf01002

[15]Field, J. (n.d.). *On a personal note: Thank you. How to Write a Thank You Note*. Retrieved July 9, 2014, from http://www.hallmark.com/thank-you/ideas/how-to-write-a-thank-you-note/

[16]List of social networking websites. (n.d.). *Wikipedia*. Retrieved July 25, 2014, from http://en.wikipedia.org/wiki/List_of_social_ networking_websites#F

[17]Devgan, S. (2021, December 9). 100 Social Media Statistics You Must Know In 2022 [+ Infographic]. Retrieved February 4, 2022, from https://statusbrew.com/insights/social-media-statistics /

[18]Clark, B. (n.d.). 22 ways to create compelling content when you don't have a clue [Infographic]. *Copyblogger*. Retrieved July 27, 2014, from http://www.copyblogger.com/create-content-info-graphic/

[19]Tugend, A. (2012, March 23). Praise is fleeting, but brickbats we recall. *The New York Times*. Retrieved July 28, 2014, from http://www.nytimes.com/2012/03/24/your-money/why-people-remember-negative-events-more-than-positive-ones.html?page-wanted=all&_r=0

[20]Geyser, W. (2021, December 29). 35 Facebook Statistics—Revenue, Users (+ Everything You Need to Know in 2022). Retrieved March 24, 2022, from https://influencermarketinghub.com/facebook-statistics/#toc-1

[21]Greenlee, M. (2021, July 28). How to create a Facebook business page, with 8 set-up tips to grow your brand. Retrieved February 27, 2022, from https://www.businessinsider.com/how-to-create-a-facebook-business-page

[22]Sponsor your page posts. Facebook. Retrieved March 3, 2022, from https://www.facebook.com/business/help/219016706130022?id=860800950779950

[23]Jay, A. Number of Twitter Users 2022/2023: Demographics, Breakdowns, & Predictions. Retrieved March 23, 2022, from https://financesonline.com/number-of-twitter-users/

[24]Hashmi, S (2022, March 10). 100+ Twitter Stats, Facts, and Insights [2022 Edition]. Retrieved March 23, 2022, from https://www.thetealmango.com/technology/twitter-stats/

[25]Fallon, J. (2013, September 24). *"#Hashtag" with Jimmy Fallon & Justin Timberlake (Late Night with Jimmy Fallon)*. YouTube. Retrieved September 27, 2014, from https://www.youtube.com/watch?v=57dzaMaouXA

[26]Andrus, A. (2014, February 17). How to spend only 10 minutes per day on Twitter. *Mashable*. Retrieved July 30, 2014, from http://mashable.com/2014/02/17/twitter-time/

[27]Gelhar, A. (2014, May 12). Student earns prom date with Texans cheerleader via Twitter. *NFL.com*. Retrieved July 31, 2014, from http://www.nfl.com/news/story/0ap2000000349753/article/student-earns-prom-date-with-texans-cheerleader-via-twitter

[28]Lin, Y. (2021, March 14). 10 LinkedIn Statistics Every Marketer Should Know in 2021 [Infographic]. Retrieved July 18, 2022 from https://www.oberlo.com/blog/linkedin-statistics#:~:text=LinkedIn %20boasts%20over%20740%20million,globe%20(LinkedIn%2C %202021)

[29]Geyser, W. (2021, December 29). LinkedIn users are more interested in your company: stats. *Econsultancy*. Retrieved March 18, 2020, from https://influencermarketinghub.com/linkedin-stats/

[30]Austin, J. (2022, January 25). *Work-Life Balance Is More Important Than Compensation in 2022, Paro Research Find*. Retrieved March 24, 2022, from https://www.businesswire.com/news/home/ 20220125005017/en/Work-Life-Balance-Is-More-Important-Than-Compensation-in-2022-Paro-Research-Finds#:~:text= Thirty%2Dnine%20percent%20of%20knowledge,were%20most %20important%20to%20them.